The Chela's Handbook

The Chela's Handbook

Compiled by

WILLIAM WILSON QUINN

TURNING
STONE
PRESS

Cover design by Frame25 Productions
Cover art by Vladimir Melnikov c/o Shutterstock.com
Interior design by Howie Severson

Turning Stone Press
8301 Broadway St., Suite 219
San Antonio, TX 78209
turningstonepress.com

Library of Congress Control Number
available upon request.

ISBN 978-1-61852-128-6

10 9 8 7 6 5 4 3 2 1

Printed in the United States of America

*For all those revered great spirits (maha ātmās),
senior and junior, whose selfless sacrifices and
singular dedication to the mission of spiritual
enlightenment of the whole of humanity have
brought them into the precinct of initiation.*

One who undertakes to try for Chelaship by that very act rouses and lashes to desperation every sleeping passion of his animal nature. For this is the commencement of a struggle for the mastery in which quarter is neither to be given nor taken. It is, once for all: "To be, or not to be"; to conquer, means ADEPTSHIP; to fail, an ignoble Martyrdom; for to fall victim to lust, pride, avarice, vanity, selfishness, cowardice, or any other of the lower propensities, is indeed ignoble, if measured by the standard of true manhood. The Chela is not only called to face all the latent evil propensities of his nature but, in addition, the whole volume of maleficent power accumulated by the community and nation to which he belongs.

—HELENA P. BLAVATSKY

Contents

Introduction

From time immemorial, the paths of those genuinely seeking higher spiritual truth have been and continue to be multiple and varied. At the beginning stages, the individual journeys of spiritual seekers typically traverse the spectrum of the world's religions and sacred societies. These journeys may often, as the wayfarer advances, include participation in active and esoterically oriented hieratic communities, such as ashrams or monasteries, under the tutelage of a resident teacher. Yet at some point, whether it be years or lifetimes from this journey's outset, depending upon the character and purity of the individual wayfarer, the opportunity to advance even farther along the spiritual path may present itself.

At this juncture, the multiple and varied spiritual paths begin to fuse and to become singular and invariable. It is as if, at the very beginning, these varied spiritual paths are at the base of a grand pyramid; and as the wayfarers who voluntarily and purposefully ascend the pyramid of spiritual truth to its higher reaches toward the narrowing apex, these inner paths necessarily draw closer together and eventually merge to become effectively *one* path. Finally, through the sacred rite of initiation, those on all spiritual paths who qualify are led to that single path whose invariable destination is the topmost point of the pyramid's apex. Upon this highest path the initiate thereafter treads solely for the benefit of humanity, thereby sacrificing his or her own release from the wheel of death and rebirth until the entirety of humanity gains its final liberation.

Those seekers of higher spiritual truth, those wayfarers, who succeed in making this climb from the base of the metaphoric spiritual pyramid to its apex will there encounter teachers—gurus—who, like themselves, also succeeded in ascending the summit of this difficult, momentous climb. These teachers are able to instruct the newly successful wayfarers in the more esoteric and extensive truths or realities of the universe, of *nature* in its totality, that may not have been accessible to their former religious or spiritual teachers who guided them at the outset of their sacred journeys. These venerable teachers form a brother/sister-hood of Adepts comprised of a diverse and extraordinarily select group of men and women that one would not ordinarily find in any orthodox religious community. Collectively, these Adepts form the *spiritual* hierarchy of humanity, having achieved highly advanced levels of spiritual awareness and capability through lifetimes of study, training, ordeal, and sacrifice. The nondenominational and eternal spiritual truths and principles taught by these Adepts are termed the *philosophia perennis* (the perennial philosophy) in Latin; this same philosophy has been expressed in Greek as *theosophia*, and in Sanskrit as the *atma-vidya*.

Access to interaction with and ultimately discipleship of these Adepts is not easy. This is because the key lies solely in the hands of the aspiring wayfarer, who *alone* must achieve an extraordinary level of purification and be endowed with an indefeasible strength and determination.

When the resolute wayfarer ascending the pyramid's apex has become spiritually pure and thoroughly selfless, and commands enough courage and strength, the way will open. This milestone is normally marked by the wayfarer formally becoming an "accepted *chela*" (Sanskrit for "pupil" or "disciple" in relation to his or her *guru*) and so beginning a personal relationship with one of the Adepts. But up to that life-changing point, one such Adept wrote, consistent with their extreme reclusiveness, that "We rarely show any outward signs by which to be recognized or sensed." Fortunately for those for whom this goal has not been realized, but for whom it may be proximate, there exists considerable guidance and instruction on how interaction with these Adepts may be commenced—and maintained.

The best of this guidance has been made available to us in modern English in the form of numerous letters handwritten by several of these Adepts to their various accepted chelas and to certain of their "lay" chelas. This remarkable correspondence occurred during the last quarter of the nineteenth century. While the recipients of these letters were many, the majority of these letters were addressed to Alfred P. Sinnett, who at the time of the commencement of this correspondence was the editor of India's largest English-language newspaper, *The Pioneer*.

The guidance and instruction by these Adepts during this period was entirely unique in recorded history, and not only those aspiring to become chelas but humanity as a whole should not fail to take full advantage of the profound truths and wisdom it contains. As the Adept Koot Hoomi wrote to his chela Francesca Arundale in 1884,

> Think you truth has been shown to you for your
> sole advantage? That we have broken the silence of

centuries for the profit of a handful of dreamers only? The converging lines of your karma have drawn each and all of you into this [Theosophical] Society as to a common focus, that you may each help to work out the results of your interrupted beginnings in the last birth (*Letters from the Masters of the Wisdom*, First Series, no. 4, p. 23).

The intercourse of the corresponding Adepts with noninitiates like Sinnett and others during this period was not only extraordinary, but was to some degree experimental based on special energies associated with a critical point in the cycle of duration. And even with the passage of time in the interim from then to now, the ultimate results of this twenty-five-year period of intercourse cannot be said to be yet fully calculated.

What follows is a compilation of select sentences and paragraphs culled from this extensive collection of letters by these Adepts—in their own thoughts and words— dealing primarily with (1) how to become and (2) how to remain a chela under their tutelage. The reader should understand at the outset, however, that at the time of their writing certain of these Adepts did not intend for their private letters to be circulated, and they at least directly counseled A. P. Sinnett, in writing, against circulating them. Regardless of this express caveat, shortly following the death of Sinnett in 1921, the Adepts' letters to him were published in London in book form by a third party, some forty years after they were written, thereby releasing them to the world.

All the letters referenced in this book were written between 1875 and 1885, and many have now been widely reproduced and in circulation for over a hundred years.

Taken as a whole, these letters are certainly educational, but they are more than merely educational. Given the historic facts of their appearance in print, it is perhaps forgivable that good—and pragmatic—use be made of them in the form of this book as a manual of sorts, as express guidance to those seeking higher spiritual truth and possibly seeking a reverential connection to these Adepts. Significantly, the Adept Koot Hoomi was generous enough to offer that "not only you [Mohini Chatterjee], a chela of mine, but anyone else is at liberty to take anything, whole pages, if thought proper, from any of my 'copied' letters." Made as an exception to the general caveat of not circulating these letters, this offer was directed to the community of spiritual aspirants then gathered within the sphere of the Adepts' influence. This offer also included, again in the Adept's words, the "liberty to even copy them verbatim and without quotation marks" (*Letters from the Masters of the Wisdom*, First Series, no. 53, pp. 112–113). Mindful of the history of the initial publication of these letters, one can choose to read the spirit of this generous permission as extending to this Adept's fellow Adepts and their handwritten letters. This choice was made here in part because such generous permission is wholly consistent with the compassion of the Adepts' collective efforts to guide and instruct those who earnestly seek, and who wish to follow the Buddhist ideal of the *bodhisattva*.

It should be noted, furthermore, that for the serious seeker this book should not be viewed as a substitute for reading the letters in their entirety, nor should one conclude that the materials selected on the topic of chelaship, being subjective, are entirely exhaustive. As with everything else on the spiritual path, a prospective chela's discovery of meaningful guidance must "be the result of one's personal merit and exertions"—a core principle in treading this higher path of which we are repeatedly reminded by the Adepts. In other words, in each seeker's reading of the entirety of these letters there may be other sentences and paragraphs that, due to timing or other relevant factors, ring particularly true to that individual at that moment, based on his or her own experiences and level of advancement on the spiritual path, and which will further propel that wayfarer toward the goal.

The material that follows is divided into topic areas in the interest of those readers who may aspire ultimately to undergo probation in order to become chelas. These five sections contain, among other things, advice pertaining to the requirement for absolute purity; the development of the intuition; the internal struggle between the chela's inner and outer persons; the development of the will; the protocols of formally becoming and remaining a chela; and the requirement of utter selflessness. The names given to these topics are not derived from the original authors of these excerpts. In addition, included with each excerpt are pertinent details of the original letter, though it should be understood that some of this information was not always provided by the authors or recorded by recipients, and is thus unavailable.

The first section deals with the perilous risks, the extraordinary difficulty, and the suffering that arise from the sacrifice of electing to begin such an arduous spiritual journey as a probationer chela of one of the Adepts, and continuing on toward initiation. This topic appears first by design, since this higher spiritual journey is not for the faint of heart, so it is better that the wayfarer knows as clearly as possible the difficulties and cumulative sacrifices involved prior to launching into it. It may be that some aspirants, through the act of rigorous and candid self-examination of their own characters and natures, will put aside the quest for chelaship once having been made aware of the arduousness of the path before them. Better that, and to progress safely upon one's own gradual spiritual journey, than to undertake such a direct and often unforgiving ascent to the summit of spiritual truth unprepared. Such an ill-considered ascent invariably leads to taking upon oneself more than one can manage, which inevitably results in unwelcome if not dire consequences. But for those who elect to proceed and attempt to surmount the forbidding obstacles, notwithstanding these grave risks and difficulties, may they become illustrious examples of the truth of the ancient maxim *palmam qui meruit ferat*: "let whoever earns the palm bear it."

W. W. Q.

A Note on Reproductions of the Letters

There have been no fewer than four separate editions of *The Mahatma Letters to A. P. Sinnett* in English, comprised of letters written to Alfred P. Sinnett by several Adepts or "Mahatmas." Most of these letters were written by the Adept known as Koot Hoomi, often through the intermediary of his accepted chelas and, on occasion and under his orders, signed by one of those chelas. A number of these letters were written by the Adept known as Morya. The majority of the letters to Sinnett were written and received between 1880 and 1885.

A. P. Sinnett died in 1921 without ever having published the many letters he received—and saved—from these Adepts, according to their express wishes. However, following his death the executor of his estate arranged through A. Trevor Barker to have the letters published. The first book edition was published in 1923, but owing to mistakes in the transcription of the letters, a second edition was published in 1926, also by Barker. Yet a third edition was published in 1962, edited by Christmas Humphreys and Elsie Benjamin. Finally, the most useful of the editions, the fourth, was published in 1993 under the meticulous arrangement of Vicente Hao Chin Jr., which placed the letters in sequence chronologically. In what follows, each excerpt will indicate, if known, (1) the recipient of the letter; (2) the author of the letter; (3) the date of the letter; and (4) the specific book, followed by the number of the letter, and the page number where the selected text begins in the edition where the reader may most conveniently find its printed reproduction in full.

In addition to those letters contained in *The Mahatma Letters to A. P. Sinnett*, there are numerous other letters written not only by the Adepts Koot Hoomi and Morya but by several other Adepts of their brotherhood. These letters, covering a span of years from 1870 to 1900, were received not only by A. P. Sinnett but by a relatively wide circle of chelas and "lay" chelas. Most of these letters appeared in print in a two-part series edited by C. Jinarajadasa titled *Letters from the Masters of the Wisdom*, "First Series" and "Second Series." The first of these series of letters was published in 1919, and has since gone through up to seven editions, and numerous printings. As time has passed, other letters written by the Adepts to their chelas have more recently come to light. A number of such letters never before reproduced in print appeared in *Mrs. Holloway and the Mahatmas*, edited by Daniel Caldwell and published in 2012.

Notwithstanding the variety of editions, printings, and publishers of these letters, the goal of this effort has been to provide the reader with a clear description of the recipients, senders, dates, and numbers of these letters that appear not only in *The Mahatma Letters to A. P. Sinnett* but also in the two volumes identified below. From among the numerous editions, printings, and publishers of *Letters from the Masters of the Wisdom*, the two principal ones employed here are those of the Theosophical Publishing House for the First Series (Adyar, 7th ed., 2011), and the Theosophical Publishing House for the Second Series

(Adyar, 4th reprint, 2002). Readers should be aware that the purposeful selection of the three separate volumes of the Adepts' letters for use in this book was based on both the availability and ease of access of these editions as convenient references for comparison to the original handwritten letters, and for further reading and study. As needed, the few excerpts used here from letters reproduced in editions other than those listed in the abbreviations will indicate those editions in full in the text, below the excerpt in question.

Finally, as the letters used in this book were all handwritten between 1875 and 1885 and thus have long been in the public domain, arguably for this reason many have been redacted and edited in the various editions and printings from multiple publishers. In light of this, and in order to conform as much as possible to scholarly standards of redaction and reproduction, every effort was made to use where possible the original handwritten versions of the letters and to use the full and correct text. Clear and operable photographic and microfilmed versions of the vast majority of these original handwritten letters from 1880 to 1885 are freely accessible and can be viewed at https://theosophy.wiki/en/Mahatma_Letters_Portal.

For the interested researcher, the majority of the letters in their original handwritten forms are preserved in archives and museums in several countries: most are in the British Museum in London; many are in the archives of the Theosophical Society in Adyar, India; others are housed in the archives of the Point Loma Theosophical Society in southern California; and others largely relating to the former chela of Koot Hoomi, Laura Holloway, are located in the Winterthur Museum in Delaware. It is also tempting to speculate, given the literary record of more than two dozen chelas who are known to have received letters from the Adepts during the late nineteenth century (and perhaps other unknown chelas who may currently receive them), how many such letters are today extant only as confidential correspondence or held in private family collections that have never been revealed to or shared with the wider public.

W. W. Q.

Abbreviations

MLS   *The Mahatma Letters to A. P. Sinnett*. Compiled and edited by Vicente Hao Chin Jr. Quezon City, Philippines: Theosophical Publishing House, 1993.

1 LMW   *Letters from the Masters of the Wisdom*, First Series. 7th edition. Compiled by C. Jinarajadasa. Adyar, India: Theosophical Publishing House, 2011.

2 LMW   *Letters from the Masters of the Wisdom*, Second Series. 4th reprint. Compiled by C. Jinarajadasa. Adyar, India: Theosophical Publishing House, 2002.

MHM   *Mrs. Holloway and the Mahatmas*. Compiled and edited by Daniel H. Caldwell. New York: Blavatsky Study Center, 2012.

KH   The Adept Koot Hoomi

M   The Adept Morya

SB   The Adept Serapis Bey

DK   The chela Djual Khul

APS   Alfred P. Sinnett

AOH   A. O. Hume

HPB   Helena P. Blavatsky

HSO   Henry S. Olcott

CWL   Charles W. Leadbeater

LCH   Laura C. Holloway

FA   Francesca Arundale

☞ 1 ☜

Sacrifice, Suffering, and Risks of the First Steps

Sigh not for chelaship; pursue not that, the dangers and hardships of which are unknown to you.

Verily many are the chelas offering themselves to us, and as many have failed this year as were accepted on probation. Chelaship unveils the inner man and draws forth the dormant vices as well as the dormant virtue. Latent vice begets active sins and is often followed by insanity. . . .

Be pure, virtuous, and lead a holy life and you will be protected. But remember, he who is not as pure as a young child better leave chelaship alone.

To: "A Member"   **From:** KH   **Date:** ca. late 1883   1 LMW no. 9, p. 33

But through her [HPB] you may be enabled to conquer the trials of initiation. They are hard and you may yet despair more than once, but do not *I pray thee*. Remember some men have toiled for years, for the knowledge you have obtained in a few months.

To: HSO   **From:** SB   **Date:** ca. 1876   2 LMW no. 10, p. 27

If you would learn and acquire Occult Knowledge, you have, my friend, to remember that such tuition opens in the stream of chelaship many an unforeseen channel to whose current even a "lay" chela must perforce yield, or else strand upon the shoals; and knowing this to abstain forever judging on mere appearance.

To: APS   **From:** KH   **Date:** ca. Summer 1884   MLS no. 134, p. 443

I have only given you a glimpse into the hell of this [unnamed] lost soul, to show you what disaster may come upon the "lay-chela" who snatches at forbidden power before his moral nature is developed to the point of fitness for its exercise. You must think well over the article "Chelas and Lay Chelas" which you will find in the *Supplement* of the July [1883] *Theosophist*.

To: APS   **From:** KH   **Date:** ca. late July 1883   MLS no. 111, p. 374

To be accepted as a chela on *probation*—is an easy thing. *To become an accepted* chela—is to court the miseries of "probation." Life in the ordinary run is not entirely made up of heavy trials and mental misery: the life of a chela who offers himself voluntarily is one long sacrifice. He, who would control hereafter the events of his life here and *beyond*, has first of all to submit himself to be controlled, yet triumph over every temptation, every woe of flesh and mind.

To: Dr. Hubbe   **From:** KH   **Date:** August 1, 1884   2 LMW no. 68, p. 124
Schleiden

I WARN you, and will say no more, apart from reminding you in a general way, that the task you are so bravely undertaking, that *Missio in partibus infidelium* ["mission in the land of the infidels"]—is the most ungrateful, perhaps, of all tasks! But, if you believe in my friendship for you, if you value the word of *honour* of one who never—*never* during his whole life polluted his lips with an untruth, then do not forget the words I once wrote to you . . . *of those who engage themselves in the occult sciences*; he who does it "must either reach the goal or *perish*. Once fairly started on the way to the great Knowledge, to doubt is to risk insanity; to come to a dead stop is to fall; to recede is to tumble backward, headlong into an abyss."

To: APS **From:** KH **Date:** February 20, 1881 MLS no. 15, p. 47

You were told, however, that the path to Occult Sciences has to be trodden laboriously and crossed at the danger of life; that every new step in it leading to the final goal is surrounded by pit-falls and cruel thorns; that the pilgrim who ventures upon it is made first to confront and conquer the thousand and one furies who keep watch over its adamantine gates and entrance—furies called Doubt, Skepticism, Scorn, Ridicule, Envy and finally Temptation—especially the latter; and that he who would see *beyond* had to first destroy this living wall; that he must be possessed of a heart and soul clad in steel, and of an iron, never-failing determination and yet be meek and gentle, humble and have shut out from his heart every human passion that leads to evil.

To: APS **From:** KH **Date:** July 18, 1884 MLS no. 126, p. 422

I shall waste no condolences upon the poor "lay-chelas" because of the "delicate weapons they can alone work with." A sorry day it would be for mankind if any sharper or deadlier ones were put in their unaccustomed hands! Ah! you would concur with me, my faithful friend, if you could but see the plaint one of them has just made on account of the agonizing results of the poisoned weapons he got the wielding of, in an evil hour, through the help of a sorcerer. Crushed morally, by his own selfish impetuosity; rotting physically from diseases engendered by the animal gratifications he snatched with "demon" help; behind him a black memory of wasted chances and hellish successes; before him a pall of dark despair—of *avitchi*—this wretched man turns his impotent rage against our "starry science" and ourselves, and hurls his ineffectual curses at those he vainly besieged for more powers in chelaship, and whom he deserted for a necromantic "Guru" who now leaves the victim to his fate. Be satisfied, friend, with your "delicate weapons"; if not as lethal as the discus of Vishnu, they can break down many barriers if plied with power. The poor wretch in question confesses to a course of "lies, breaches of faith, hatreds, temptings or misleading of others, injustices, calumnies, perjuries, false pretenses," etc. The "risk" he "voluntarily took," but he adds, "if *they* (we) had been good and kind as well as wise and powerful, they (we) *would have certainly prevented me* from undertaking a task to which they knew I was unequal." In a word, we, who have gained our knowledge, such as it is, by the only practicable method, and who have no right to hinder any fellow man from making the attempt (though we have the right to warn, and we *do* warn every candidate), we are expected to take upon our own heads the penalty of such interference, or try to save ourselves from the same by making incompetents into adepts in spite of themselves! Because *we* did not do this, he is "left to linger out a wretched existence as an animated poison bag, full of mental, moral, and physical corruption."

To: APS   **From:** KH   **Date:** ca. July 1883   MLS no. 111, p. 373

Ah, how long shall the mysteries of chelaship overpower and lead astray from the path of truth the wise and perspicacious, as much as the foolish and the credulous! How few of the many pilgrims who have to start without chart or compass on that shoreless Ocean of Occultism reach the wished for land. Believe me, faithful friend, that *nothing* short of full confidence in us, in our good motives if not in our wisdom, in our foresight, if not omniscience— which is not to be found on this earth—can help one to cross over from one's land of dream and fiction to our Truth land, the region of stern reality and fact. Otherwise the ocean will prove shoreless indeed; its waves will carry one no longer on waters of hope, but will turn every ripple into doubt and suspicion; and bitter shall they prove to him who starts on that dismal, tossing sea of the Unknown, with a prejudiced mind!

To: APS   **From:** KH   **Date:** ca. Summer 1884   MLS no. 134, p. 440

My dear friend, I strongly advise you not to undertake at present a task beyond your strength and means; for once pledged were you to break your promise it would cut you off for years, if not forever from any further progress.

To: APS   **From:** KH   **Date:** unknown   MLS no. 59, p. 155

The poor boy [Damodar Mavalankar] has had his fall. Before he could stand in the presence of the "Masters" he had to undergo the severest trials that a neophyte ever passed through, to atone for the many questionable doings in which he had over-zealously taken part, bringing disgrace upon the sacred science and its adepts. The mental and physical suffering was too much for his weak frame, which has been quite prostrated, but he will recover in course of time. **This ought to be a warning to you all.** [Emphasis added.] You have believed "not wisely but too well." To unlock the gates of the mystery you must not only lead a life of the strictest probity, but learn to discriminate truth from falsehood. You have talked a great deal about karma but have hardly realized the true significance of that doctrine.

To: HSO   **From:** KH   **Date:** June 5, 1884   1 LMW no. 29, p. 70

When you open M.'s letter of 1881 you will find the key to many mysteries—this included. Intuitive as you naturally are—*chelaship* is yet almost a complete puzzle for you as for my friend Sinnett, and the others, they have scarcely an inkling of it yet. Why must I even now—(to put your thoughts in the right channel) remind you of the three cases of insanity within seven months among "lay chelas," not to mention one's turning a thief? Mr. Sinnett may consider himself lucky that his *lay chelaship* is in "fragments" only, and that I have so uniformly discouraged his desires for a closer relationship as an *accepted* chela. Few men know their inherent capacities—only the ordeal of crude chelaship develops them. (Remember these words: they have a deep meaning.)

To: HSO   **From:** KH   **Date:** ca. June 1883   MLS no. 110, p. 371

❧ 2 ❧

Probation Before Chelaship
and Its Tests and Trials

Do not imagine that which cannot be; do not hope that at the last moment you will be helped. If you are unfit to pass your first probation and assert your rights of a future Adept by forcing circumstances to bow before you—you are as totally unfit for any further trials.

To: HSO   **From:** M   **Date:** June 11, 1879   2 LMW no. 27, p. 69

But be warned, my friend, that this is not the last of your probations. It is not I who create them, but *yourself*—by your struggle for light and truth against the world's dark influences. Be more careful as to what you say upon forbidden topics.

To: APS   **From:** KH   **Date:** October 8, 1883   MLS no. 114, p. 393

Well, this suspicion led me to think that one so high in a Society *that neither tolerates nor practices deceit*, could not much care to belong to our poor Brotherhood *that does both*—regarding its probationists. Hence—my silence.

To: E. W. Fern   **From:** M   **Date:** ca. Fall 1882   2 LMW no. 75, p. 143

Thus, little by little, the now incomprehensible will become the self-evident; and many a sentence of mystic meaning will shine yet out before your Soul-eye, like a transparency, illuminating the darkness of your mind. Such is the course of gradual progress.

To: APS   **From:** KH   **Date:** March 3, 1882   MLS no. 49, p. 140

The degree of success or failure [in probation] *are the landmarks we shall have to follow, as they will constitute the barriers placed with your own hands between yourselves and those whom you have asked to be your teachers. The nearer your approach to the goal contemplated, the shorter the distance between the student and the Master.* [Emphasis in original.]

To: Unknown   **From:** unknown   **Date:** ca. 1885   2 LMW no. 82, p. 159
                        via HPB

I am afraid the "poor, dear Mrs. Holloway" is showing her white teeth and would hardly be found now "a charming companion." . . . It is Fern, Moorad Ali, Bishen Lal and other wrecks, over again. Why will "would-be" *chelas* with such intense self personalities, force themselves within the enchanted and dangerous circle of probation!

To: APS   **From:** KH   **Date:** ca. Summer 1884   MLS no. 128, p. 429

The Chela "on probation" is like the wayfarer in the old fable of the sphinx; only the one question becomes a long series of every day riddles propounded by the Sphinx of Life, who sits by the wayside, and who, unless her ever changing and perplexing puzzles are successfully answered one after the other, impedes the progress of the traveler and finally destroys him.

To: Dr. Hubbe   **From:** KH   **Date:** August 1, 1884   2 LMW no. 68, p. 124
   Schleiden

If, throwing aside every preconceived idea, you could TRY and impress yourself with this profound truth that intellect is not all powerful by itself; that to become "a mover of mountains" it has first to receive life and light from its higher principle—Spirit, and then would fix your eyes upon everything occult, spiritually trying to develop the faculty according to the rules, then you would soon read the mystery right.

To: APS   **From:** KH   **Date:** July 18, 1884   MLS no. 126, p. 426

The mass of human sin and frailty is distributed throughout the life of man who is content to remain an average mortal. It is gathered in and centred, so to say, within one period of the life of a chela—the period of probation. That which is generally accumulating to find its legitimate issue only in the next rebirth of an ordinary man, is quickened and fanned into existence in the chela—especially in the presumptuous and selfish candidate who rushes in without having calculated his forces.

To: APS   **From:** KH   **Date:** November 8, 1884   MLS no. 134, p. 441

He who would shorten the years of probation has to make sacrifices for theosophy. Pushed by malevolent hands to the very edge of a precipice, the Society needs every man and woman strong in the cause of truth. It is by *doing* noble actions and not by only determining that they shall be done that the fruits of the meritorious actions are reaped. Like the "true man" of Carlyle who is not to be seduced by ease—"difficulty, abnegation, martyrdom, death are the *allurements* that act" during the hours of trial on the heart of a *true* chela.

To: CWL   **From:** KH   **Date:** October 31, 1884   1 LMW no. 7, p. 31

Chelaship is an educational as well as probationary stage and the chela alone can determine whether it shall end in adeptship or failure. Chelas from a mistaken idea of our system too often watch and wait for orders, wasting precious time which should be taken up with personal effort. Our cause needs missionaries, devotees, agents, even martyrs perhaps. But it cannot demand of any man to make himself either. So now choose and grasp your own destiny, and may our Lord's the Tathagata's memory aid you to decide for the best.

To: CWL   **From:** KH   **Date:** October 31, 1884   1 LMW no. 7, p. 32

You laugh at *probations*—the word seems ridiculous as applied to you? You forget that he who approaches our precincts even in thought, is drawn into the vortex of probation. At any rate your temple totters, and unless you put your strong shoulders against its wall you may share the fate of Samson. Pride and "dignified contempt" will not help you in the present difficulties. There is such a thing—when understood allegorically—as treasures guarded by faithful gnomes and fiends. The treasure is our occult knowledge that many of you are after.

To: APS   **From:** KH   **Date:** October 10, 1884   MLS no. 131, p. 435

You ask me —"what rules I must observe during this time of probation, and how soon I might venture to hope that it could begin." I answer: you *have* the making of your own future, in your own hands as shown above, and every day you may be weaving its woof. If I were to *demand* that you should do one thing or the other, instead of simply advising, I would be responsible for every effect that might flow from the step and you acquire but a secondary merit. Think, and you will see that this is true.

To: CWL   **From:** KH   **Date:** October 31, 1884   1 LMW no. 7, p. 31

Verily "suspicion overturns, what confidence builds"! And if, on the one hand, you have some reasons to quote Bacon against us, and say that "there is nothing that makes a man suspect much, more than to know little," on the other hand you ought also to remember that our Knowledge and Science cannot be pursued altogether on the Baconian methods. We are not permitted—come what may—to offer it as a remedy against, or to cure people from suspicion. They have to earn it for themselves, and he who will not find our truths in his soul and within himself—has poor chances of success in Occultism.

To: APS   **From:** KH   **Date:** July 18, 1884   MLS no. 126, p. 425

The option of receiving him or not as a regular chela—remains with the Chohan. M. has simply to have him tested, tempted and examined by all and every means, so as to have his real nature drawn out. This is a rule with us as inexorable as it is disgusting in your Western sight, and I could not prevent it even if I would. It is not enough to know thoroughly what the chela is capable of doing or not doing at the time and under the circumstances during the period of probation. We have to know of what he *may* become capable under different and every kind of opportunities. Our precautions are all taken.

To: APS   **From:** KH   **Date:** ca. August 1882   MLS no. 74, p. 227

The probations are hard all round and are sure not to meet your European notions of truthfulness and sincerity. But reluctant as I do feel to use such means or even to permit them to be used in connection with *my chelas*, yet I must say that the deception, the lack of good faith, and the *traps* (!!) intended to inveigle the Brothers, have multiplied so much of late; and there is so little time left to that day that will decide the selection of the *chelas*, that I cannot help thinking that our chiefs and especially M. may be after all right. With an enemy one has to use either equal or better weapons. But do not be deceived by appearance.

To: APS   **From:** KH   **Date:** August 22, 1882   MLS no. 78, p. 241

[I] must remind you of that which you so heartily hate; namely, that no one comes in contact with us, no one shows a desire to know more of us, but has to submit to being tested and put by us on probation. Thus, C.C.M[assey]. could no more than any other escape his fate. He has been tempted and allowed to be deceived by appearances, and to fall but too easily a prey to his weakness—suspicion and lack of self-confidence. In short, he is found wanting in the first element of success in a candidate—*unshaken faith*, once that his conviction rests upon, and has taken root in knowledge, not simple belief in certain facts.

To: APS   **From:** KH   **Date:** ca. October 1882   MLS no. 92, p. 294

The pathway through earth-life leads through many conflicts and trials, but he who does naught to conquer them can expect no triumph. Let then the anticipation of a fuller introduction into our mysteries under more congenial circumstances, the creation of which depends *entirely upon yourself* inspire you with patience to wait for, perseverance to press on to, and full preparation to receive the blissful consummation of all your desires. And for that you have to remember that when K.H. shall say to you, Come up hither—you should be ready. Otherwise the all powerful hand of our Chohan will appear once more between you and *Him*.

To: APS   **From:** M   **Date:** ca. February 1882   MLS no. 43, p. 117

The process of self-purification is not the work of a moment, nor of a few months but of years—nay, extending over a series of lives. The later a man begins the living of a higher life, the longer must be his period of probation, for he has to undo the effects of a long number of years spent in objects diametrically opposed to the real goal. The more strenuous his efforts and the brighter the result of his work, the nearer he comes to the threshold. If his aspiration is genuine—a settled conviction and not a sentimental flash of the moment—he transfers from one body to another the determination which finally leads him to the attainment of his desire.

To: Pandit   **From:** KH   **Date:** ca. January 1884   1 LMW no. 6, p. 28
Pran Nath

True, you have been labouring for the cause without remission for many months and in many directions; but you must not think that because *we have never shown any knowledge of what you have been doing*, nor that, because we have never acknowledged or thanked you for it in our letters—that we are either ungrateful for, or ignore purposely or otherwise what you have done, for it is really not so. For, though no one ought to be expecting thanks for doing his duty by humanity and the cause of truth—since, after all, he who labours for others, labours but for himself—nevertheless, my Brother I feel deeply grateful to you for what you have done.

To: AOH   **From:** KH   **Date:** ca. August 1882   MLS no. 74, p. 229

I now answer the above and your other questions.

(1) It is *not* necessary that one should be in India during the seven years of probation. A *chela* can pass them anywhere. (2) To accept any man as a chela does not depend on my personal will. It can only be the result of one's personal merit and exertions in that direction. *Force* any one of the "Masters" you may happen to choose; do good works in his name and for the love of mankind; be pure and resolute in the path of righteousness (as laid out in *our* rules); be honest and unselfish; forget your *Self* but to remember the good of other people—and you will have *forced* that "Master" to accept you.

To: CWL   **From:** KH   **Date:** October 31, 1884   1 LMW no. 7, p. 30

However well fitted psychically and physiologically to answer such selection, unless possessed of spiritual, as well as of physical unselfishness a chela whether selected or not, must perish, as a chela in the long run. Self personality, vanity and conceit harboured in the higher principles are enormously more dangerous than the same defects inherent only in the lower physical nature of man. They are the breakers against which the cause of chelaship, in its probationary stage, is sure to be dashed to pieces unless the would-be disciple carries with him the white shield of perfect confidence and trust in those he would seek out through mount and vale to guide him safely toward the light of Knowledge.

To: APS   **From:** KH   **Date:** November 8, 1884   MLS no. 134, p. 441

Such a development of your psychical powers of hearing, as you name—the Siddhi of hearing occult sounds—would not be at all the easy matter you imagine. It was never done to any one of us, for the iron rule is that what powers one gets *he must himself acquire.* And when acquired and ready for use the powers lie dumb and dormant in their potentiality like the wheels and clockwork inside a musical box; and only then does it become easy to wind up the key and set them in motion. . . . Yet every earnestly disposed man *may* acquire such powers practically. That is the finality of it; there are no more distinctions of persons in this than there are as to whom the sun shall shine upon or the air give vitality to. There are the powers of all nature before you; *take what you can.*

To: AOH   **From:** KH   **Date:** June 30, 1882   MLS no. 65, p. 169

A chela under probation is allowed to think and do whatever he likes. He is warned and told beforehand: "You will be tempted and deceived by appearances; two paths will be open before you, both leading to the goal you are trying to attain; one easy, and that will lead you more rapidly to the fulfilment of orders you may receive; the other—more arduous, more long; a path full of stones and thorns that will make you stumble more than once on your way; and, at the end of which you may, perhaps, find failure after all and be unable to carry out the orders given for some particular small work—but, whereas the latter will cause the hardships you have undergone on it to be all carried to the side of your credit in the long run, the former, the easy path, can offer you but a momentary gratification, an easy fulfilment of the task."

The chela is at perfect liberty, *and often quite justified from the standpoint of appearances*—to suspect his Guru of being "a fraud" as the elegant word stands. More than that: the greater, the sincerer his indignation—whether expressed in words or boiling in his heart—the more fit he is, the better qualified to become an *adept*. He is free to use, and will not be held to account for using the most abusive words and expressions regarding his guru's actions and orders, provided he comes out victorious from the fiery ordeal; provided he resists all and every temptation; rejects every allurement, and proves that nothing, not even the promise of that which he holds dearer than life, of that most precious boon, his future adeptship—is able to make him deviate from the path of truth and honesty, or force him to become a *deceiver*.

To: AOH   **From:** KH   **Date:** ca. August 1882   MLS no. 74, p. 222

Every human being contains within himself vast potentialities, and it is the duty of the adepts to surround the would-be chela with circumstances which shall enable him to take the "right-hand path"—if he have the ability in him. We are no more at liberty to withhold the chance from a postulant than we are to guide and direct him into the proper course. At best, we can only show him—after his probation period was successfully terminated—that if he does this he will go right; if the other, wrong. But until he has passed that period, we leave him to fight out his battles as best he may; and have to do so occasionally with higher and *initiated* chelas such as H.P.B., once they are allowed to work in the world, that all of us more or less avoid. More than that . . . we allow our candidates *to be tempted* in a thousand various ways, so as to draw out the whole of their inner nature and allow it the chance of remaining conqueror either one way or the other.

To: APS   **From:** KH   **Date:** ca. October 1882   MLS no. 92, p. 299

You must thoroughly put aside the personal element if you would get on with occult study and—for a certain time—even with himself. Realize, my friend, that the social affections have little, if any, control over any true adept in the performance of his duty. In proportion as he rises towards perfect adeptship the fancies and antipathies of his former self are weakened: (as K.H. in substance explained to you) he takes all mankind into his heart and regards them in the mass. Your case is an exceptional one. You have *forced* yourself upon him [KH], and stormed the position, by the very violence and intensity of your feeling for him—and once he accepted he has to bear the consequences in the future. Yet it cannot be a question with him what the visible Sinnett may be— what his impulses, his failures or successes in his world, his diminished or undiminished regard for him. With the "visible" one we have nothing to do. He is to us only a veil that hides from profane eyes that other ego with whose evolution we are concerned.

To: APS   **From:** M   **Date:** ca. January 1882   MLS no. 42, p. 112

❧ 3 ❧

Qualities and Behaviors
Necessary for Advancement

We have one word for all aspirants: TRY.

To: APS   **From:** KH   **Date:** March 18, 1882   MLS no. 54, p. 148

Our greatest trouble is to teach pupils not to be befooled by appearances.

To: APS   **From:** M   **Date:** ca. February 1882   MLS no. 42, p. 113

"To dare, to will, to act and remain silent" is our motto as that of every Kabalist and Occultist.

To: R. Keshava Pillai   **From:** KH   **Date:** ca. 1882   2 LMW no. 65, p. 118

Motive is everything and man is punished in a case of *direct* responsibility, never otherwise.

To: APS   **From:** KH   **Date:** August 1882   MLS no. 70-C, p. 213

You have to make once for ever your choice—either your duty to the Lodge or your own personal ideas.

To: HSO   **From:** Narayan   **Date:** ca. 1876   2 LMW no. 24, p. 52

Intentions—you may tell your fellow-members—and kind words count for little with us. Deeds—is what we want and demand.

To: FA   **From:** KH   **Date:** ca. Fall 1884   1 LMW no. 4, p. 22

One who would have higher instruction given to him has to be a *true* theosophist in heart and soul, not merely in appearance.

To: APS   **From:** KH   **Date:** October 10, 1884   MLS no. 131, p. 437

Remember that no effort is ever lost, and that for an occultist there is no past, present or future, but ever an *Eternal Now.*

To: Damodar   **From:** KH   **Date:** February 27, 1884   1 LMW no. 27, p. 68
    Mavalankar

The greatest consolation in and the foremost duty of life, child, is not to give pain, and avoid causing suffering to man or beast.

To: LCH   **From:** KH   **Date:** October 2, 1884   1 LMW no. 36, p. 78

Happy is he who crosses the great gulf between *himself* and us—unscared with doubt and free from the pollution of suspicion.

To: Ramaswami **From:** M **Date:** ca. February 1883 2 LMW no. 54, p. 101
Iyer

As Mr. Sinnett rightly says in his *Esoteric Buddhism*, the higher spiritual progress must be accompanied by intellectual development on a parallel line.

To: Damodar **From:** KH **Date:** February 27, 1884 1 LMW no. 27, p. 68
Mavalankar

Spiritual faculties demand instruction and regulation even more than our mental gifts, for intellect imbibes wrong far more easily than good.

To: LCH **From:** KH **Date:** July 1884 1 LMW no. 33, p. 76

Occult Science is a jealous mistress and allows not a shadow of self-indulgence; and it is "fatal" not only to the ordinary course of married life but even to flesh and *wine* drinking.

To: APS **From:** KH **Date:** ca. June 1882 MLS no. 62, p. 161

Learn first our laws and educate your perceptions, dear Brother. Control your involuntary powers and develop in the right direction your will and you will become a teacher instead of a learner.

To: AOH **From:** KH **Date:** October 1882 MLS no. 90, p. 285

So long as one has not developed a perfect sense of justice, he should prefer to err rather on the side of mercy than commit the slightest act of injustice.

To: Franz   **From:** KH   **Date:** ca. February 1884   2 LMW no. 73, p. 131
Hartmann

In our sight there is no crime worse than ingratitude and injustice; and to see one who suffers them without protest is equal to seeing in him a passive confederate to them.

To: HPB   **From:** KH   **Date:** ca. 1888   1 LMW no. 60, p. 126

Be true, be loyal to your pledges, to your sacred duty, to your country, to your own conscience. Be tolerant to others, respect the religious views of others if you would have your own respected.

To: T. S.   **From:** KH   **Date:** December 1883   1 LMW no. 2, p. 12
Convention
Members

I can do nothing, if she [LCH] does not help me by helping herself. Try to make her realize that in occultism one can neither go back nor stop, that an abyss opens behind every step taken forward.

To: HPB   **From:** KH   **Date:** ca. Summer 1884   1 LMW no. 39, p. 82

One who becomes a slave to any physical weakness never becomes the master of even the lower powers of nature. Be patient, content with little and—*never ask for more* if you would hope to ever get it.

To: W. T. Brown   **From:** KH   **Date:** December 17, 1883   1 LMW no. 22, p. 62

[H]e who is desirous to learn how to benefit humanity, and believes himself able to read the characters of other people, must begin first of all, *to learn to know himself*, to appreciate his own character at its true value.

To: APS and AOH   **From:** M   **Date:** October 1881   MLS no. 29, p. 89

Courage and fidelity, truthfulness and sincerity, always win our regard. Keep on, child, as you have been doing. Fight for the persecuted and the wrong, those who thro' self-sacrifice have made themselves *helpless* whether in Europe or China.

To: LCH   **From:** KH   **Date:** ca. Summer 1884   1 LMW no. 41, p. 85

Those who pause and hesitate and are the most cautious before entering into the spirit of an entirely new scheme are to be generally far more relied upon than those who rush into every new enterprise like so many flies into a bowl of boiling milk.

To: HPB   **From:** M   **Date:** May 19, 1880   2 LMW no. 31, p. 73

The term "Universal Brotherhood" is no idle phrase. Humanity in the mass has a paramount claim upon us . . . It is the only secure foundation for universal morality. If it be a dream, it is at least a noble one for mankind: and it is the aspiration of the *true adept*.

To: APS **From:** KH **Date:** November 3, 1880 MLS no. 5, p. 20

He who damns himself in his own estimation and agreeably to the recognized and current code of honour to save a worthy cause may some day find out that he has reached thereby his loftiest aspirations. Selfishness and the want of self-sacrifice are the greatest impediments on the path of adeptship.

To: Mohini Chaterjee **From:** KH **Date:** unknown 1 LMW no. 10, p. 34

The degree of diligence and zeal with which the hidden meaning is sought by the student, is generally the test—how far he is entitled to the possession of the so buried treasure. And certainly if you were able to make out [through intuition] that which was concealed under the red ink of M.—you need despair of nothing.

To: APS **From:** KH **Date:** March 3, 1882 MLS no. 49, p. 141

He who hears his brother reviled, and keeping a smooth face leaves the abuse unnoticed, tacitly agrees with the enemy, as if he admitted the same to be proper and just. He who does it is either mouse-hearted, or selfishness is at the bottom of his heart. He is not fit as yet to become a "companion." [Quoted in full by SB, from the *Dhammapada*, Verse XXII]

To: HSO   From: SB   Date: August 16, 1876   2 LMW no. 23, p. 48

Perhaps you will better appreciate our meaning when told that in our view the highest aspirations for the welfare of humanity become tainted with selfishness if, in the mind of the philanthropist, there lurks the shadow of desire for self-benefit or a tendency to do injustice, even when these exist unconsciously to himself.

To: APS   From: KH   Date: October 19, 1880   MLS no. 2, p. 8

Ever turn away your gaze from the imperfections of your neighbour and centre rather your attention upon your own shortcomings in order to correct them and become wiser . . . Show not the disparity between claim and action in another man but, whether he be brother or neighbour, rather help him in his arduous walk in life.

To: Unknown   From: Unknown   Date: ca. 1885   2 LMW no. 82, p. 158

But my first duty is to *my* Master. And duty, let me tell you, is for us, stronger than friendship or even love; as with this abiding principle which is the indestructible cement that has held together for so many milleniums, the scattered custodians of nature's grand secrets—our Brotherhood, nay, our doctrine itself—would have crumbled long ago into unrecognizable atoms.

To: APS   **From:** KH   **Date:** July 18, 1884   MLS no. 126, p. 422

My chelas must never doubt, nor suspect, nor injure our agents by foul thoughts. Our modes of action are strange and unusual and but too often liable to create suspicion. The latter is a snare and a temptation. Happy is he, whose spiritual perceptions ever whisper truth to him! Judge those directly concerned with us by that perception, not according to your worldly notions of things.

To: Mohini   **From:** KH   **Date:** ca. September 1882   2 LMW no. 58,
Chatterjee   p. 106

To all, whether Chohan or chela, who are obligated workers among us the first and last consideration is whether we can do good to our neighbour, no matter how humble he may be; and we do not permit ourselves to even think of the danger of any contumely, abuse or injustice visited upon ourselves. We are ready to be "spat upon and crucified" daily—not once—if real good to another can come of it.

To: APS   **From:** KH   **Date:** October 8, 1883   MLS no. 114, p. 392

A higher faculty belonging to the higher life must see, and it is truly impossible to force it upon one's understanding—merely in words. One must see with his spiritual eye, hear with his Dharmakayic ear, feel with the sensations of his *Ashta-vijñāna* (spiritual "I") before he can comprehend this doctrine fully; otherwise it may but increase one's "discomfort," and add to his knowledge very little.

To: APS   **From:** KH   **Date:** February 2, 1883   MLS no. 104, p. 362

It is not enough that you should set the example of a pure, virtuous life and a tolerant spirit; this is but negative goodness—and for *chelaship* will never do. You should, even as a simple member, much more as an officer, learn that you may teach, acquire spiritual knowledge and strength that the work may lean upon you, and the sorrowing victims of ignorance learn from you the cause and remedy of their pain.

To: FA   **From:** KH   **Date:** ca. Fall 1884   1 LMW no. 4, p. 19

As a bystander and a deeply interested one, I only discern somewhat of the truth that is hidden in the hearts of all of you. Are all of you sincere in your promises? Take care lest rashly made promises broken should turn back on you and thus become your greatest punishment. Be true, sincere and faithful. Work for the cause and our blessings will ever be upon you. Doubt and forget your sacred promises and—in the darkness of guilt and sorrow will ye repent.

To: R. Keshava Pillai   **From:** KH   **Date:** ca. 1882   2 LMW no. 64, p. 115

For he who hopes to solve in time the great problems of the Macrocosmal World and conquer face to face the Dweller, taking thus by violence the threshold on which lie buried nature's most mysterious secrets, must Try, first, the energy of his Will power, the indomitable resolution to succeed, and bringing out to light all the hidden mental faculties of his Atma and highest intelligence, get at the problems of Man's Nature and solve first the mysteries of his heart.

To: HSO   **From:** SB   **Date:** June 25, 1875   2 LMW no. 16, p. 38

Look around you, my friend: see the "three poisons" raging within the heart of men—anger, greed, delusion, and the five obscurities: envy, passion, vacillation, sloth, and unbelief—ever preventing them seeing truth. They will never get rid of the pollution of their vain, wicked hearts, nor perceive the spiritual portion of themselves. Will you not try—for the sake of shortening the distance between us—to disentangle yourself from the net of life and death in which they are all caught, to cherish less— lust and desire?

To: APS   **From:** KH   **Date:** ca. February 1882   MLS no. 47, p. 129

He who would lift up high the banner of mysticism and proclaim its reign near at hand, must give the example to others. He must be the first to change *his* modes of life; and, regarding the study of the occult mysteries as the upper step in the ladder of Knowledge must loudly proclaim it such despite exact science and the opposition of society. "The Kingdom of Heaven is obtained by force" say the Christian mystics. It is but with armed hand, and ready to either conquer or perish that the modern mystic can hope to achieve his object.

To: APS   **From:** KH   **Date:** October 19, 1880   MLS no. 2, p. 7

Please then, remember, what she [HPB] tried to explain, and what you gathered tolerably well from her, namely the fact of the *seven* principles in the *complete* human being. Now, no man or woman, unless he be an initiate of the "fifth circle," can leave the precincts of *Bod-Lhas* and return back into the world in his integral whole—if I may use the expression. *One* at least of his seven satellites has to remain behind for two reasons; the first to form the necessary connecting link, the wire of transmission— the second as the safest warranter that certain things will never be divulged.

To: AOH   **From:** KH   **Date:** ca. Fall 1881   MLS no. 22, p. 79

For our doctrines to practically react on the so-called moral code, or the ideas of truthfulness, purity, self-denial, charity, etc., we have to preach & popularize a knowledge of Theosophy. It is not the individual and determined purpose of attaining oneself Nirvana (the culmination of all knowledge and absolute wisdom) which is after all only an exalted and glorious *selfishness*—but the self-sacrificing pursuit of the best means to lead on the right path our neighbour, to cause as many of our fellow-creatures as we possibly can to benefit by it, which constitutes the true Theosophist.

To: APS and AOH   **From:** The Mahachohan   **Date:** late 1881   1 LMW no. 1, p. 4

"Nothing was ever lost by trying." You share with all beginners the tendency to draw too absolutely strong inferences from partly caught hints, and to dogmatize thereupon as though the last word had been spoken. You will correct this in due time. You may misunderstand us, are more than likely to do so, for our language must always be more or less that of parable and suggestion, when treading upon forbidden ground; we have our own peculiar modes of expression and what lies behind the fence of words is even more important than what you read. But still—TRY.

To: APS   **From:** KH   **Date:** ca. July 1883   MLS no. 111, p. 380

I will begin by reminding you, that at different times, especially during the last two months, you have repeatedly offered yourself as a *chela*, and the first duty of one is to hear without anger or malice anything the guru may say. How can we ever *teach* or you *learn* if we have to maintain an attitude utterly foreign to us and our methods—that of two society men? If you really want to be a *chela*, i.e., to become the recipient of our mysteries, *you* have to adapt yourself to *our* ways, not we to *yours*. Until you do so, it is useless for you to expect any more than we can give under ordinary circumstances.

To: AOH   **From:** KH   **Date:** ca. August 1882   MLS no. 74, p. 225

Those who are carried away by phenomena are generally the ones who being under the domain of Maya are thus unable and incompetent to study or understand the philosophy. Exhibition of phenomena in such cases is not only a waste of power, but positively injurious. In some it encourages superstition, while in others it develops the latent germ of hostility towards philanthropists who would resort to such phenomena being shown. Both the extremes are prejudicial to real human progress which is happiness. For a time wonders may attract a mob, but that is no step towards the regeneration of humanity.

To: Navatamram   **From:** KH   **Date:** March 1884   1 LMW no. 44, p. 100
   Ootamram

It is but a truism, yet I say it, that in adversity alone can we discover the real man. It is a true manhood when one boldly accepts one's share of the collective karma of the group one works with, and does not permit oneself to be embittered, and to see others in blacker colours than reality, or to throw all blame upon some one "black sheep," a victim, specially selected. Such a true man as that we will ever protect and, despite his shortcomings, assist to develop the good he has in him. Such an one is sublimely *unselfish*; he sinks his personality in his cause, and takes no heed of discomforts or personal obloquy unjustly fastened upon him.

To: APS   **From:** KH   **Date:** October 10, 1884   MLS no. 131, p. 437

Now the lake in the mountain heights of your being is one day a tossing waste of waters, as the gust of caprice or temper sweeps through your soul; the next a mirror as they subside and peace reigns in the "house of life." One day you win a step forward; the next you fall two back. Chelaship admits none of these transitions; its prime and constant qualification is a calm, even, contemplative state of mind (not the mediumistic passivity) fitted to receive psychic impressions from without, and to transmit one's own from within. The mind can be made to work with electric swiftness in a high excitement; but the Buddhi—never. To its clear region, calm must ever reign.

To: LCH   **From:** KH   **Date:** August 22, 1884   1 LMW no. 30, p. 72

There is one general law of vision (physical and mental or spiritual) but there is a qualifying special law proving that all vision must be determined by the quality or grade of man's spirit and soul, and also by the ability to translate diverse qualities of waves of astral light into consciousness. There is but one general law of life, but innumerable laws qualify and determine the myriads of forms perceived and of sounds heard . . . Unless regularly initiated and trained—concerning the spiritual insight of things and the supposed revelations made unto man in all ages from Socrates down to Swedenborg and "Fern"—no self-tutored seer or clairaudient ever saw or heard *quite* correctly.

To: APS   **From:** M   **Date:** ca. November 1881   MLS no. 31, p. 98

In our mountains here, the Dugpas lay at dangerous points, in paths frequented by our Chelas, bits of old rag, and other articles best calculated to attract the attention of the unwary, which have been impregnated with their evil magnetism. If one be stepped upon a tremendous psychic shock may be communicated to the wayfarer, so that he may lose his footing and fall down the precipice before he can recover himself. Friend, beware of Pride and Egoism, two of the worst snares for the feet of him who aspires to climb the high paths of Knowledge and Spirituality. You have opened a joint of your armour for the Dugpas—do not complain if they have found it out and wounded you there.

To: APS   **From:** KH   **Date:** October 10, 1884   MLS no. 131, p. 436

How can you know the real from the unreal, the true from the false? Only by self-development. How get that? By first carefully guarding yourself against the causes of self-deception. And this you can do by spending a certain fixed hour or hours each day all alone in self-contemplation, writing, reading, the purification of your motives, the study and correction of your faults, the planning of your work in the external life. These hours should be sacredly reserved for this purpose, and no one, not even your most intimate friend or friends, should be with you then. Little by little your sight will clear, you will find the mists pass away, your interior faculties strengthen, your attraction towards us gain force, and certainty replace doubts.

To: LCH   **From:** KH   **Date:** August 22, 1884   1 LMW no. 31, p. 74

But for the attainment of your proposed object, viz., for a clearer comprehension of the extremely abstruse and at first incomprehensible theories of our occult doctrine, never allow the serenity of your mind to be disturbed during your hours of literary labour, nor before you set to work. It is upon the serene and placid surface of the unruffled mind that the visions gathered from the invisible find a representation in the visible world. Otherwise you would vainly seek those visions, those flashes of sudden light which have already helped to solve so many of the minor problems and which alone can bring the truth before the eye of the soul. It is with jealous care that we have to guard our mind-plane from all the adverse influences which daily arise in our passage through earth-life.

To: AOH   **From:** KH   **Date:** June 30, 1882   MLS no. 65, p. 169

Fasting, meditation, chastity of thought, word, and deed; silence for certain periods of time to enable nature herself to speak to him who comes to her for information; government of the animal passions and impulses; utter unselfishness of intention, the use of certain incense and fumigations for physiological purposes, have been published as the means since the days of Plato and Iamblichus in the West and since the far earlier times of our Indian *Rishis*. How these must be complied with to suit each individual temperament is of course a matter for his own experiment and the watchful care of his tutor or *Guru*. Such is in fact part of his course of discipline, and his Guru or initiator can but assist him with his experience and will power but can do no *more until the last and Supreme initiation*.

To: APS   **From:** KH   **Date:** August 5, 1881   MLS no. 20, p. 73

Why must you be so faint-hearted in the performance of your duty? Friendship, personal feelings, and gratitude are no doubt noble feelings, but duty alone leads to the development you so crave for.

To: LCH   **From:** KH   **Date:** ca. Summer 1884   1 LMW no.34, p. 77

The victor's crown is only for him who proves himself worthy to wear it; for him who attacks Mara single handed and conquers the demon of lust and earthly passions; and not we but he himself puts it on his brow. It was not a meaningless phrase of the Tathagata that "he who masters Self is greater than he who conquers thousands in battle": there is no such other difficult struggle. If it were not so, adeptship would be but a cheap acquirement . . . One who is true and approved to-day, may to-morrow prove, under a new concatenation of circumstances a traitor, an ingrate, a coward, an imbecile. The reed, bent beyond its limit of flexibility, will have snapped in twain. Shall we accuse it? No; but because we can, and do pity it, we cannot select it as part of those reeds that have been tried and found strong, hence fit to be accepted as material for the indestructible fane we are so carefully building.

To: APS   **From:** KH   **Date:** ca. October 1882   MLS no. 92, p. 299

Beware then, of an uncharitable spirit, for it will rise up like a hungry wolf in your path, and devour the better qualities of your nature that have been springing into life. Broaden instead of narrowing your sympathies; try to identify yourself with your fellows, rather than to contract your circle of affinity.

To: APS   **From:** KH   **Date:** October 10, 1884   MLS no. 131, p. 435

It is useless for a member to argue "I am one of a pure life, I am a teetotaller and an abstainer from meat and vice. All my aspirations are for good, etc." and he, at the same time, building by his acts and deeds an impassable barrier on the road between himself and us. What have we, the disciples of the true *Arhats*, of esoteric Buddhism and of Sang-gyas to do with the *Shastras* and Orthodox Brahmanism? There are 100 of thousands of Fakirs, Sannyasis and Sadhus leading the most pure lives, and yet being as they are, on the path of *error*, never having had an opportunity to meet, see or even hear of us. Their forefathers have driven away the followers of the only true philosophy upon earth from India and now it is not for the latter to come to them but for them to come to us if they want us. Which of them is ready to become a Buddhist, a *Nastika* as they call us? None. Those who have believed and followed us have had their reward.

To: APS   **From:** M via HPB   **Date:** November 4, 1881   MLS no. 30, p. 95

Learn, child, *to catch a hint through whatever agency it may be given.* "Sermons may be preached even through stones."

To: LCH   **From:** KH   **Date:** ca. Spring 1884   1 LMW no. 31, p. 75

Once separated from the common influences of society, nothing draws us to any outsider save his evolving spirituality. He may be a Bacon or an Aristotle in knowledge, and still not even make his current felt a feather's weight by us, if his power is confined to the Manas [mind]. The supreme energy resides in the Buddhi; latent—when wedded to *Atman* alone, active and irresistible when galvanized by the *essence* of "Manas" and when none of the dross of the latter commingles with that pure essence to weigh it down by its finite nature. *Manas*, pure and simple, is of a lower degree, and of the earth earthly: and so your greatest men count but as nonentities in the arena where greatness is measured by the standard of spiritual development. When the ancient founders of your philosophical schools came East, to acquire the lore of our predecessors, they filed no claims, except the single one of a sincere and *unselfish* hunger for the truth.

To: APS   **From:** KH   **Date:** ca. July 1883   MLS no. 111, p. 375

The situation is this: men who join the [Theosophical] Society with the one selfish object of reaching power, making occult science their only or even chief aim may as well not join it—they are doomed to disappointment as much as those who commit the mistake of letting them believe that the Society is nothing else. It is just because they preach too much "the Brothers" and too little if at all *Brotherhood* that they fail. How many times had we to repeat, that he who joins the Society with the sole object of coming in contact with us and if not of acquiring at least of assuring himself of the reality of such powers and of our objective existence—was pursuing a mirage? I say again then. It is he alone who has the love of humanity at heart, who is capable of grasping thoroughly the idea of a regenerating practical Brotherhood who is entitled to the possession of our secrets. He alone, such a man—will never misuse his powers, as there will be no fear that he should turn them to selfish ends. A man who places not the good of mankind above his own good is not worthy of becoming our *chela*—he is not worthy of becoming higher in knowledge than his neighbour.

To: APS **From:** M **Date:** ca. December 1881 MLS no. 33, p. 100

Does it seem to you a small thing that the past year has been spent only in your "family duties"? Nay, but what better cause for reward, what better discipline, than the daily and hourly performance of duty? Believe me my "pupil," the man or woman who is placed by Karma in the midst of small plain duties and sacrifices and loving-kindness, will through these faithfully fulfilled rise to the larger measure of Duty, Sacrifice and Charity to all Humanity—what better path towards the enlightenment you are striving after than the daily conquest of Self, the perseverance in spite of want of visible psychic progress, the bearing of ill-fortune with that serene fortitude which turns it to spiritual advantage—since good and evil are not to be measured by events on the lower or physical plane. Be not discouraged that your practice falls below your aspirations, yet be not content with *admitting* this, since you clearly recognise that your tendency is too often towards mental and moral indolence, rather inclining to drift with the currents of life, than to steer a direct course of your own. Your spiritual progress is far greater than you know or can realize, and you do well to believe that such development is *in itself* more important than its realization by your physical plane consciousness.

To: APS   **From:** KH   **Date:** unknown   MLS no. 123, p. 419

≈ 4 ≈

The Adepts and Their Practices and Rules

One who prepares for solving the *Infinite* must solve the *finite* first.

To: HSO   **From:** Serapis Bey   **Date:** ca. 1876   2 LMW no. 18, p. 41

Every step made by one in our direction will force us to make one toward him.

To: APS   **From:** KH   **Date:** ca. Spring 1885   MLS no. 136, p. 452

[W]e recognise but one law in the Universe, the law of harmony, of *perfect* EQUILIBRIUM.

To: AOH   **From:** KH   **Date:** October 1882   MLS no. 90, p. 282

Nothing, my friend—even apparently absurd and reprehensible actions—is done by us without a purpose.

To: APS   **From:** KH   **Date:** January 6, 1883   MLS no. 101, p. 345

Of course you know . . . that when we take *candidates* for chelas, they take the vow of secrecy and silence respecting every order they may receive. One has to prove himself fit for *chelaship*, before he can find out whether he is fit for *adeptship*.

To: APS   **From:** KH   **Date:** August 23, 1882   MLS no. 75, p. 231

It is esoteric philosophy alone, the spiritual and psychic blending of man with Nature, that, by revealing fundamental truths, can bring that much desired mediate state between the two extremes of human Egotism and divine Altruism, and finally lead to the alleviation of human suffering.

To: Unknown   **From:** Unknown   **Date:** ca. 1885   2 LMW no. 82, p. 157

We never whine over the inevitable but try to make the best of the worst. And though we neither push nor draw into the mysterious domain of occult nature those who are unwilling; never shrink from expressing our opinions freely and fearlessly, yet we are ever as ready to assist those who come to us.

To: APS   **From:** KH   **Date:** October 29, 1880   MLS no. 5, p. 19

The laws which govern our Lodge will not allow us to interfere with her [HPB's] fate, by means that might seem supernal.

To: HSO   **From:** SB   **Date:** ca. 1876   2 LMW no. 9, p. 25

The only object to be striven for is the amelioration of the condition of MAN by the spread of truth suited to the various stages of his development and that of the country he inhabits and belongs to. TRUTH has no ear-mark and does not suffer from the name under which it is promulgated—if the said object is attained.

To: APS and From: KH **Date:** December 7, 1883 MLS no. 120, p. 410
    Others

Please realize the fact that so long as men doubt there will be curiosity and enquiry, and that enquiry stimulates reflection which begets effort; but let our secret be once thoroughly vulgarized and not only will skeptical society derive no great good but our privacy would be constantly endangered and have to be continually guarded at an unreasonable cost of power.

To: APS and AOH **From:** M **Date:** ca. October 1881 MLS no. 29, p. 93

Every Western theosophist should learn and remember, especially those of them who would be our followers—that in our Brotherhood all personalities sink into one idea—abstract right and absolute practical justice for all. And that, though we may not say with the Christians, "return good for evil"—we repeat with Confucius, "return good for good; for evil—JUSTICE."

To: London Lodge **From:** KH **Date:** January 1884 MLS no. 120, p. 412

The doctrine we promulgate being the only true one, must—supported by such evidence as we are preparing to give become ultimately triumphant as every other truth. Yet it is absolutely necessary to inculcate it gradually, enforcing its theories, unimpeachable facts for those who know, with direct inferences deduced from and corroborated by the evidence furnished by modern exact science.

To: APS and AOH   **From:** The Mahachohan   **Date:** late 1881   1 LMW no. 1, p. 3

But remember: we are not public scribes or clerks, with time to be continually writing notes and answers to individual correspondents about every trifling personal matter that they should answer for themselves. Nor shall we permit those private notes to be forwarded as freely as hitherto. Time enough to *discuss* the terms of chelaship when the aspirant has digested what has already been given out, and mastered his most palpable vices and weaknesses.

To: FA   **From:** KH   **Date:** ca. Fall 1884   1 LMW no. 4, p. 21

But above all, good and faithful friend, do not allow your self to misconceive the real position of our Great Brotherhood. Dark and tortuous as may seem to your Western mind the paths trodden, and the ways by which our candidates are brought to the great Light—you will be the first to approve of them when you know *all*. Do not judge on appearances—for you may thereby do a great wrong, and lose your own personal chances to learn more. Only be vigilant and—watch.

To: APS   **From:** KH   **Date:** August 23, 1882   MLS no. 75, p. 236

Both of you labour under the strange impression that *we can*, and even *do* care for anything that may be said or thought of us. Disabuse your minds, and remember that the first requisite in even a simple fakir, is that he should have trained himself to remain as indifferent to moral pain as to physical suffering. Nothing can give US *personal* pain or pleasure. And what I now say is, rather to bring you to understand US than *yourselves* which is the most difficult science to learn.

To: APS and AOH   **From:** M   **Date:** ca. October 1881   MLS no. 29, p. 91

In common with many, you blame us for our great secrecy. Yet we know something of human nature, for the experience of long centuries—aye, ages—has taught us. And we know, that so long as science has anything to learn, and a shadow of religious dogmatism lingers in the hearts of the multitudes, the world's prejudices have to be conquered step by step, not at a rush. As hoary antiquity had more than one Socrates so the dim Future will give birth to more than one martyr.

To: APS   **From:** KH   **Date:** October 15, 1880   MLS no. 1, p. 4

We, my dear sirs, always judge men by their motives and the moral effects of their actions: for the world's false standards and prejudice we have no respect.

To: APS   **From:** KH   **Date:** ca. July 1883   MLS no. 112, p. 384

The abundance of MSS. from me of late shows that I have found a little leisure; their blotched, patchy and mended appearance also proves that my leisure has come by snatches, with constant interruptions, and that my writing has been done in odd places here and there, with such materials as I could pick up. But for the RULE that forbids our using one minim of power until every ordinary means has been tried and failed, I might, of course, have given you a lovely "precipitation" as regards chirography and composition.

To: APS   **From:** KH   **Date:** ca. July 1882   MLS no. 68, p. 203

The mysteries never were, never can be, put within the reach of the general public, not, at least, until that longed for day when our religious philosophy becomes universal. At no time have more than a scarcely appreciable minority of men possessed nature's secret, though multitudes have witnessed the practical evidences of the possibility of their possession. The adept is the rare efflorescence of a generation of enquirers; and to become one, he must obey the inward impulse of his soul irrespective of the prudential considerations of worldly science or sagacity.

To: APS   **From:** KH   **Date:** October 19, 1880   MLS no. 2, p. 6

But beware of seeking or leaning too much upon direct authority. *Our* ways are not your ways. We rarely show any outward signs by which to be recognized or sensed.

To: LCH   **From:** KH   **Date:** ca. Spring 1884   1 LMW no. 31, p. 74

If, for generations we have "shut out the world from the Knowledge of our Knowledge," it is on account of its absolute unfitness; and if, notwithstanding proofs given, it still refuses yielding to evidence, then will we at the End of this cycle retire into solitude and our kingdom of silence once more. . . . We have offered to exhume the primeval strata of man's being, his basic nature, and lay bare the wonderful complications of his inner Self— something never to be achieved by physiology or even psychology in its ultimate expression—and demonstrate it scientifically.

To : APS   **From:** KH   **Date:** July 5, 1881   MLS no.18, p. 68

And we have but to bear in mind the recent persecutions of mediums in England, the burning of supposed witches and sorcerers in South America, Russia and the frontiers of Spain—to assure ourselves that the only salvation of the genuine proficients in occult sciences lies in the skepticism of the public: the charlatans and the jugglers are the natural shields of the "adepts." The public safety is only ensured by our keeping secret the terrible weapons which might otherwise be used against it, and which, as you have been told became deadly in the hands of the wicked and selfish.

To: APS   **From:** KH   **Date:** October 17, 1880   MLS no. 1, p. 4

The Adepts and Their Practices and Rules   49

Believe me: we may yet walk along the arduous path together. We may yet meet: But if at all, it has to be along and *on*—those "adamantine rocks with which our occult rules surround us"—never *outside* them, however bitterly we may complain. No, *never* can we pursue our further journey—*if* hand in hand—along that high-way, crowded thoroughfare, which encircles them, and on which Spiritualists and mystics, prophets and seers elbow each other now-a-day. Yea, verily, the motley crowd of candidates may shout for an eternity to come, for the *Sesame* to open. It never will, so long as they keep outside those rules.

To: APS   **From:** KH   **Date:** March 3, 1882   MLS no. 49, p. 136

The first and most important of our objections [to making public appearances] is to be found in our *Rules*. True, we have our schools and teachers, our neophytes and shaberons (superior adepts), and the door is always opened to the right man who knocks. And we invariably welcome the new comer; only, instead of going over to him he has to come to us. More than that; unless he has reached that point in the path of occultism from which return is impossible, by his having irrevocably pledged himself to our association, we never—except in cases of utmost moment—visit him or even cross the threshold of his door in visible appearance.

To: APS   **From:** KH   **Date:** October 19, 1880   MLS no. 2, p. 8

Thus, a good thought is perpetuated as an active beneficent power; an evil one as a maleficent demon. And so
man is continually peopling his current in space with a
world of his own, crowded with the offspring of his fancies, desires, impulses, and passions, a current which
reacts upon any sensitive or and [sic] nervous organiza-
tion which comes in contact with it in proportion to its
dynamic intensity. The Buddhist calls this his "Skan-
dha," the Hindu gives it the name of "Karma"; the Adept
evolves these shapes consciously, other men throw them
off unconsciously.

The adept to be successful and preserve his power must
dwell in solitude and more or less within his own soul.

To: AOH   **From:** KH   **Date:** November 1, 1880   MLS Appendix no. 1,
p. 472

When our great Buddha—the patron of all the adepts, the
reformer and the codifier of the occult system, reached
first *Nirvana* on earth, he became a Planetary Spirit; i.e.—
his spirit could at one and the same time rove the inter-
stellar spaces *in full consciousness*, and continue at will on
Earth in his original and individual body. For the divine
Self had so completely disfranchised itself from matter
that it could create at will an inner substitute for itself,
and leaving it in the human form for days, weeks, sometimes years, affect in no wise by the change either the
vital principle or the physical mind of its body. By the
way, that is the highest form of adeptship man can hope
for on our planet.

To: APS   **From:** KH   **Date:** July 5, 1881   MLS no. 18, p. 62

One does not cease entirely, my dear friend to be a *man* nor lose one's dignity for being an *adept*. In the latter capacity, one, no doubt, remains in every case quite indifferent to the opinion of the outside world. The former always draws the line between *ignorant surmise* and—deliberate, *personal insult*. I cannot really be expected to take advantage of the first to be ever hiding the problematic "adept" behind the skirts of the two supposed "humourists" and as *man*, I had too much experience lately in such above said insults with Messrs. S. Moses and C.C. Massey to give them any more opportunities to doubt the word of "K.H.," or see in him a vulgar defendant, a kind of guilty, tricky Babu before a panel of stern European jurymen and Judge.

To: APS   **From:** KH   **Date:** ca. December 1883   MLS no. 117, p. 402

To be *true*, religion and philosophy must offer the solution of every problem. That the world is in such a bad condition morally is a conclusive evidence that none of its religions and philosophies, those of the *civilized* races less than any other, have ever possessed the *truth*. The right and logical explanations on the subject of the problems of the great dual principles, right and wrong, good and evil, liberty and despotism, pain and pleasure, egotism and altruism, are as impossible to them now as they were 1881 years ago. They are as far from the solution as they ever were, but—to these there *must* be somewhere a consistent solution, and if our doctrines prove their competence to offer it, then the world will be quick to confess that must be the true philosophy, the true religion, the true light, which gives *truth* and nothing but the *truth*.

To: APS and   **From:** The Mahachohan   **Date:** late 1881   1 LMW no. 1, p. 11
    AOH

The human brain is an exhaustless generator of the most refined quality of cosmic force, out of the low, brute energy of nature; and the complete adept has made himself a centre from which irradiate potentialities that beget correlations upon correlations through Æons to come. This is the key to the mystery of his being able to project into and materialise in the visible world the forms that his imagination has constructed out of inert cosmic matter in the invisible world. The adept does not create anything new, but only utilises and manipulates materials which nature has in store around him; a material which throughout eternities has passed through all the forms; he has but to choose the one he wants and recall it into objective existence.

To: AOH   **From:** KH   **Date:** November 1, 1880   MLS Appendix no. 1, p. 471

Plato was right: *ideas* rule the world; and, as men's minds will receive *new* ideas, laying aside the old and effete, the world will advance; mighty revolutions will spring from them; creeds and even powers will crumble before their onward march crushed by the irresistible force. It will be just as impossible to resist their influx, when the time comes, as to stay the progress of the tide. But all this will come gradually on, and before it comes we have a duty set before us; that of sweeping away as much as possible the dross left to us by our pious forefathers. New ideas have to be planted on clean places, for these ideas touch upon the most momentous subjects. It is not physical phenomena but these universal ideas that we study, as to comprehend the former, we have to first understand the latter.

To: APS   **From:** KH   **Date:** December 10, 1880   MLS no. 12, p. 39

The world—meaning that of individual existences—is full of those latent meanings and deep purposes which underlie all the phenomena of the Universe, and Occult Sciences—i.e., *reason* elevated to supersensuous Wisdom—can alone furnish the key wherewith to unlock them to the intellect. Believe me, there comes a moment in the life of an adept, when the hardships he has passed through are a thousandfold rewarded. In order to acquire further knowledge, he has no more to go through a minute and slow process of investigation and comparison of various objects, but is accorded an instantaneous, implicit insight into every first truth. Having passed that stage of philosophy which maintains that all fundamental truths have sprung from a blind impulse . . . the adept sees and feels and lives in the very source of all fundamental truths—the Universal Spiritual Essence of Nature, SHIVA the Creator, the Destroyer, and the Regenerator.

To: APS   **From:** KH   **Date:** March 26, 1881   MLS no. 17, p. 55

I, am as I was; and, as I was and am, so am I likely always to be—the slave of my duty to the Lodge and mankind; not only taught, but desirous to subordinate every preference for individuals to a love for the human race.

To: APS and AOH   **From:** M   **Date:** ca. October 1881   MLS no. 29, p. 92

The degrees of an Adept's initiation mark the seven stages at which he discovers the secret of the sevenfold principles in nature and man and awakens his dormant powers.

To: AOH   **From:** KH   **Date:** July 10, 1882   MLS no. 67, p. 189

As the course of the river depends upon the nature of its basin, so the channel for communication of Knowledge must conform itself to surrounding circumstances. The Egyptian Hierophant, the Chaldean Mage, the Arhat, and the Rishi, were bound in days of yore on the same voyage of discovery and ultimately arrived at the same goal though by different tracks. There are even at the present moment three centres of the Occult Brotherhood in existence, widely separated geographically, and as widely *exoterically*—the true esoteric doctrine being identical in substance though differing in terms; all aiming at the same grand object, but no two agreeing *seemingly* in the details of procedure. It is an every day occurrence to find students belonging to different schools of occult thought sitting side by side at the feet of the same Guru. *Upasika* (Madam B.) and Subba Row, though pupils of the same Master, have not followed the same Philosophy—the one is Buddhist and the other an Adwaitee.

To: London Lodge   **From:** KH   **Date:** January 1884   MLS no. 120, p. 410

We refuse no one. "Spheres of usefulness" can be found everywhere. The *first* object of the Society is philanthropy. The true theosophist is the Philanthropist who— "not for himself, but for the world he lives."

To: Dr. Hubbe   **From:** KH   **Date:** August 1, 1884   2 LMW no. 68, p. 125
    Schleiden

The major and minor yugas must be accomplished according to the established order of things. And we, borne along on the mighty tide, can only modify and direct some of its minor currents. If we had the powers of the imaginary Personal God, and the universal and immutable laws were but toys to play with, then indeed might we have created conditions that would have turned this earth into an Arcadia for lofty souls. But having to deal with an immutable Law, being ourselves its creatures, we have had to do what we could and rest thankful. There have been times when "a considerable portion of enlightened minds" were taught in our schools. Such times there were in India, Persia, Egypt, Greece and Rome. But, as I remarked in a letter to Mr. Sinnett, the adept is the efflorescence of his age, and comparatively few ever appear in a single century. Earth is the battle ground of moral no less than of physical forces; and the boisterousness of animal passions under the stimulus of the rude energies of the lower group of etheric agents, always tends to quench spirituality.

To: AOH   **From:** KH   **Date:** November 1, 1880   MLS Appendix no. 1, p. 474

You ought to have learned by this time our ways. We *advise*—and never *order*. But we *do* influence individuals.

To: APS   **From:** M   **Date:** March 3, 1882   MLS no. 48, p. 134

The Occult Science is *not* one in which secrets can be communicated of a sudden, by a written or even verbal communication. If so, all the "Brothers" would have to do, would be to publish a *Hand-book* of the art which might be taught in schools as grammar is. It is the common mistake of people that we willingly wrap ourselves and our powers in mystery—that we wish to keep our knowledge to ourselves, and of our own will refuse— "wantonly and deliberately" to communicate it. The truth is that till the neophyte attains to the condition necessary for that degree of Illumination to which, and for which, he is entitled and fitted, most *if not all* of the Secrets are *incommunicable*. The receptivity must be equal to the desire to instruct. The illumination *must come from within*. Till then no hocus pocus of incantations, or mummery of appliances, no metaphysical lectures or discussions, no self-imposed penance can give it. All these are but means to an end, and all we can do is to direct the use of such means as have been empirically found by the experience of ages to conduce to the required object. And this was and has been *no secret* for thousands of years.

To: APS   **From:** KH   **Date:** August 5, 1881   MLS no. 20, p. 72

The fact is, that to the last and supreme initiation every chela—(and even some adepts)—is left to his own device and counsel. We have to fight our own battles, and the familiar adage—"the adept *becomes*, he is not *made*" is true to the letter. Since every one of us is the *creator* and producer of the *causes* that lead to such or some other *results*, we have to reap but what we have sown. *Our chelas are helped but when they are innocent of the causes that lead them into trouble*; when such causes are generated by foreign, outside influences. Life and the struggle for adeptship would be too easy, had we all scavengers behind us to sweep away the *effects* we have generated through our own rashness and presumption. Before they are allowed to go into the world they—the chelas—are every one of them endowed with more or less clairvoyant powers; and, with the exception of that faculty that, unless paralyzed and watched would lead them perchance to divulge certain secrets that must not be revealed—they are left in the full exercise of their powers—whatever these may be: why don't they exercise them? Thus, step by step, and after a series of punishments, is the chela taught by bitter experience to suppress and guide his impulses; he loses his rashness, his self-sufficiency and never falls into the same errors.

To: APS   **From:** KH   **Date:** ca. October 1882   MLS no. 92, p. 294

The world of force is the world of Occultism and the only one whither the highest initiate goes to probe the secrets of being. Hence no one but such an initiate can know anything of these secrets. Guided by his Guru the chela first discovers this world, then its laws, then their centrifugal evolutions into the world of matter. To become a perfect adept takes him long years, but at last he becomes the master. The hidden things have become patent, and mystery and miracle have fled from his sight forever. He sees how to guide force in this direction or that—to produce desirable effects. The secret chemical, electric or odic properties of plants, herbs, roots, minerals, animal tissue, are as familiar to him as the feathers of your birds are to you. No change in the etheric vibrations can escape him. He applies his knowledge, and behold a miracle! And he who started with the repudiation of the very idea that miracle is possible, is straightaway classed as a miracle worker and either worshiped by the fools as a demi-god or repudiated by still greater fools as a charlatan! And to show you how exact a science is occultism let me tell you that the means we avail ourselves of are all laid down for us in a code as old as humanity to the minutest detail, but everyone of us has to begin from the beginning, not from the end. Our laws are as immutable as those of Nature, and they were known to man an eternity before this strutting game-cock, modern science, was hatched.

To: AOH   **From:** KH   **Date:** ca. October 1882   MLS no. 90, p. 284

Doubt not, my friend: it is but from the very top of those "adamantine rocks" of ours [rules of the Brotherhood], not at their foot, that one is ever enabled to perceive the *whole* Truth, by embracing the whole limitless horizon. And though they may seem to you to be standing in your way, it is simply because you have hitherto failed to discover or even so much as suspect the reason and the operation of those laws; hence they appear so cold and merciless and selfish in your sight; although yourself have intuitionally recognised in them the outcome of ages of wisdom. Nevertheless, were one but to obediently follow them out, they could be made to gradually yield to one's desire and give to him *all* he asks of them. But no one could ever violently break them, without becoming the first victim to his guilt; yea, to the extent of risking to lose his own, his hard won share of immortality, *here* and *there*. Remember: too anxious expectation is not only tedious, but dangerous too. Each warmer and quicker throb of the heart wears so much of life away. The passions, the affections are not to be indulged in by him who seeks TO KNOW; for they "wear out the earthly body with their own secret power; and he, who would gain his aim—*must be cold.*" He must not even desire too earnestly or too passionately the object he would reach: else, the very wish will prevent the possibility of its fulfilment, at best—retard and throw it back. . . .

To: APS   **From:** KH   **Date:** March 3, 1882   MLS no. 49, p. 136

But, I am not quite sure that your parting remark as to our not being *invulnerable* as a body is quite free of that spirit which animated the retreating Parthians. Be it as it may, we are content to live as we do—unknown and undisturbed by a civilization which rests so exclusively upon intellect. Nor do we feel in any way concerned about the revival of our ancient arts and high civilization, for these are as sure to come back in their time, and in a higher form as the Plesiosaurus and the Megatherium in theirs. We have the weakness to believe in ever recurrent cycles and hope to *quicken* the resurrection of what is past and gone. We *could not* impede it even if we would. The "new civilization" will be but the child of the old one, and we have but to leave the eternal law to take its own course to have our dead ones come out of their graves; yet, we are certainly anxious to hasten the welcome event. Fear not; although we do "cling superstitiously to the relics of the Past" our knowledge will not pass away from the sight of man. It is the "gift of the gods" and the most precious relic of all. The keepers of the sacred Light did not safely cross so many ages but to find themselves wrecked on the rocks of modern scepticism. Our pilots are too experienced sailors to allow us [to] fear any such disaster. We will always find volunteers to replace the tired sentries, and the world, bad as it is in its present state of transitory period, can yet furnish us with a few men now and then.

To: AOH   **From:** KH   **Date:** ca. December 1880   MLS no. 11, p. 35

The Adepts and Their Practices and Rules   61

While the facilities of observation secured to some of us by our condition certainly give a greater breadth of view, a more pronounced and impartial, as a more widely spread humaneness—for answering Addison, we might justly maintain that it *is* "the business of 'magic' to humanise our natures with compassion" for the whole mankind as all living beings, instead of concentrating and limiting our affections to one predilected race—yet few of us (except such as have attained the final negation of Moksha) can so far enfranchise ourselves from the influence of our earthly connection as to be insusceptible in various degrees to the higher pleasures, emotions, and interests of the common run of humanity. Until final emancipation reabsorbs the *Ego*, it *must* be conscious of the purest sympathies called out by the esthetic effects of high art, its tenderest cords respond to the call of the holier and nobler *human* attachments. Of course, the greater the progress towards deliverance, the less this will be the case, until, to crown all, human and purely individual personal feelings—blood-ties and friendship, patriotism and race predilection—all will give away, to become blended into one universal feeling, the only true and holy, the only unselfish and Eternal one—Love, an Immense Love for humanity—as a *Whole*! For it is "Humanity" which is the great Orphan, the only disinherited one upon this earth, my friend. And it is the duty of every man who is capable of an unselfish impulse to do something, however little, for its welfare.

To: APS   **From:** KH   **Date:** February 20, 1881   MLS no. 15, p. 48

At this stage of our correspondence, misunderstood as we generally seem to be, even by yourself, my faithful friend, it may be worth our while and useful for both, that you should be posted on certain facts—and very important facts—connected with adeptship. Bear in mind then, the following points.

(1) An adept—the highest as the lowest—is one *only during the exercise of his occult powers.*

(2) Whenever these powers are needed, the sovereign will unlocks the door to the *inner* man (the adept), who can emerge and act freely but on condition that his jailor—the *outer* man—will be either completely or partially paralyzed as the case may require; viz.: either *(a)* mentally and physically; *(b)* mentally, but not physically; *(c)* physically but not entirely mentally; *(d)* neither, but with an akasic film interposed between the *outer* and the *inner* man.

(3) The smallest exercise of occult powers then, as you will now see, requires an effort. We may compare it to the inner muscular effort of an athlete preparing to use his physical strength. As no athlete is likely to be always amusing himself at swelling his veins in anticipation of having to lift a weight, so no adept can be supposed to keep his will in constant tension and the *inner* man in full function, when there is no immediate necessity for it. When the *inner* man rests the adept becomes an ordinary man, limited to his physical senses and the functions of his physical brain. Habit sharpens the intuition of the latter, yet is unable to make them supersensuous. The inner adept is ever ready, ever on the alert, and that suffices for our purposes. At moments of rest then, his faculties are at rest also.

To: APS   **From:** KH   **Date:** ca. September 1882   MLS no. 85B, p. 257

⇜ 5 ⇝

Relationships Between
Adepts and Chelas

You will not be unwatched and uncared for, but you have
to attract not to repel us and our chelas.

To: LCH   **From:** KH   **Date:** August 22, 1884   MHM no. 21, p. 123

He who seeks us finds *us*. TRY. Rest thy mind—banish all
foul doubt. We keep watch over our faithful soldiers.

To: HSO   **From:** SB   **Date:** ca. June 1875   2 LMW no. 3, p. 11

One of the Mahatmas has, within the year, written—
"Never thrust yourself upon us for Chelaship; wait until it
descends upon you."

To: Unknown   **From:** Unknown   **Date:**   H. P. Blavatsky
                              via HPB   ca. 1884   Collected Writings,
                                          vol. 6, 1883–1885, p. 286

Blind are they who see and perceive not. Their karma is spun; but what Masters can or *shall* help those who refuse to help themselves.

To: HSO　　**From:** M　　**Date:** ca. Fall 1884　　2 LMW no. 26, p. 65

Strong will creates and sympathy attracts even adepts, whose laws are antagonistic to their mixing with the uninitiated.

To: APS　　**From:** KH　　**Date:** December 1, 1880　　MLS no. 10, p. 27

I can come nearer to you, but you must draw me by a purified heart and a gradually developing will. Like the needle the adept follows his attractions.

To: APS　　**From:** KH　　**Date:** February 1882　　MLS no. 47, p. 130

Do not be too eager for "instructions" any of you. You will always get what you need as you shall deserve them, but no more than you deserve or are able to assimilate.

To: LCH　　**From:** KH　　**Date:** August 22, 1884　　1 LMW no. 31, p. 75

He who does mischief whether consciously or unconsciously without repairing it can hardly hope to win the good opinion of Maha Sahib [Serapis Bey]—least of all his favour.

To: HSO　　**From:** M　　**Date:** June 12, 1883　　2 LMW no. 41, p. 83

However little you may seem to achieve—psychically—in this birth, remember that your interior growth proceeds every instant, and that toward the end of your life as in your next birth your accumulated merit shall bring you all you aspire to.

To: APS   **From:** KH   **Date:** February 7, 1884   MLS no. 121, p. 414

[Y]ou have a letter from me in which I explain *why* we never *guide* our chelas (the most advanced even); nor do we forewarn them, leaving the effects produced by causes of their own creation to teach them better experience. Please bear in mind that particular letter.

To: APS   **From:** KH   **Date:** ca. November 1882   MLS no. 95, p. 333

If she [LCH] has not learnt yet the fundamental principle in occultism that every idle word is recorded as well as one full of earnest meaning, she ought to be told as much, before being allowed to take one step further.

To: HPB   **From:** KH   **Date:** ca. Spring 1884   1 LMW no. 39, p. 81

She [LCH] suffers, and patience was never a word for her. She would be made a regular chela before she showed herself fit even for a probationary candidate. "I am not a chela," she keeps on saying, ignorant of having pledged herself as one unconsciously and when out of the body.

To: HPB   **From:** KH   **Date:** ca. Spring 1884   1 LMW no. 39, p. 82

You cannot successfully resist fate. Are you ready to do your part in the great work of philanthropy? You have offered yourself for the Red Cross; but, Sister, there are sicknesses and wounds of the Soul that no Surgeon's art can cure. Shall you help us teach mankind that the soul-sick must heal themselves?

To: Mary   **From:** M   **Date:** August 30, 1884   2 LMW no. 72, p. 129
    Gebhard

Know, then, that even the chelas of the same guru are often made to separate and keep apart for long months while the process of development is going on—simply on account of the two contrary magnetisms that, attracting each other, prevent mutual and INDIVIDUALIZED development in some one direction.

To: APS   **From:** KH   **Date:** ca. September 1884   MLS no. 129, p. 430

I protest most emphatically against the woman [HPB] being dealt with so uncharitably. She had no intention to deceive—unless withholding a fact be a direct deceit and *lie*, on the theory *suppressio veri, suggestio falsi*—a legal maxim which she knows nothing about. But then on this theory we all (Brothers and Chelas) ought to be regarded *as liars*.

To: APS   **From:** KH   **Date:** ca. July 1883   MLS no. 112, p. 383

I am also to tell you that in a certain Mr. Bennett of America who will shortly arrive at Bombay, you may recognise one who, in spite of his national provincialism that you so detest, and his too infidelistic bias, is one of our agents (unknown to himself) to carry out the scheme for the enfranchisement of Western thoughts from superstitious creeds.

To: APS   **From:** DK   **Date:** ca. January 1882   MLS no. 37, p. 106

I will not claim my right to "unswerving obedience" in everything concerning his [A. P. Sinnett's] spiritual progress. I never do; I will simply retire from this arena of quiproquos and stubborn opposition and say no more . . . We have no time to lose in feeble controversies: either you desire further development under our guidance, or you do not.

To: LCH   **From:** KH   **Date:** early August 1884   M HM no. 17, p. 105

[M]an, after all, is the victim of his surroundings while he lives in the atmosphere of society. We may be anxious to befriend such as we have an interest in, and yet be as helpless to do so, as is one who sees a friend engulfed in a stormy sea when no boat is near to be launched and his personal strength is paralysed by a stronger hand that keeps him back.

To: APS   **From:** KH   **Date:** February 1882   MLS no. 47, p. 130

A band of students of the Esoteric Doctrines, who would reap any profits spiritually must be in perfect harmony and unity of thought. Each one individually and collectively has to be *utterly unselfish*, kind and full of good will towards each other at least—leaving humanity out of the question; there must be no party spirit among the band, no backbiting, no ill will, or envy or jealously, contempt or anger. What hurts one ought to hurt the other—that which rejoices A must feel with pleasure B.

To: HPB   **From:** M   **Date:** ca. Fall 1884   1 LMW no. 3, p. 15

But it is just because the principle has to work both ways, that . . . we feel and would have it known that we have no right to influence the free will of the members in this or any other matter. Such interference would be in flagrant contradiction to the basic law of esotericism that personal psychic growth accompanies *pari passu* the development of individual effort, and is the evidence of acquired personal merit.

To: London   **From:** KH via   **Date:** February 7, 1884   MLS no. 122,
    Lodge   Bhola Sarma   p. 417

If he [HSO] is "ignorant" of many things, so are his accusers, and because he remains still *uninitiated* the reason for which is very plain: to this day he has *preferred* the *good* of the many *to his own personal benefit*. Having given up the advantages derived from steady, serious chelaship by those who devote themselves to it, for his work for other people—*these are those who now turn against him*.

To: HSO   **From:** M   **Date:** ca. Fall 1884   2 LMW no. 26, p. 63

The Chela's Handbook

I have laboured for more than a quarter of a century night and day to keep my place within the ranks of that invisible but ever busy army which labours and prepares for a task which can bring no reward but the consciousness that we are doing our duty to humanity; and, meeting you on my way I have tried to—do not fear,—not to enroll you, for that would be impossible, but to simply draw your attention, excite your curiosity if not your better feelings to the one and only truth.

To: APS   **From:** KH   **Date:** March 26, 1881   MLS no. 17, p. 55

On your last tour you have been given so many chances for various reasons—we do not do so much (or so little if you prefer) even for our chelas, until they reach a certain stage of development necessitating no more use and abuse of power to communicate with them. If an Eastern, especially a Hindu, had even half a glimpse but once of what you had, he would have considered himself blessed the *whole of his life.*

To: W. T. Brown   **From:** KH   **Date:** December 17, 1883   1 LMW no. 22, p. 60

The deduction of Mr. Massey that "the adept foresight was not available" in sundry noted cases of theosophical failure is but the restatement of the old error that the selections of members and the actions of Founders and Chelas are controlled by us! This has been often denied, and—as I believe—sufficiently explained to you in my Darjeeling letter, but objectors cling to their theory despite all. We have no concern with, nor *do we guide the events generally.*

To: APS   **From:** KH   **Date:** ca. January 1883   MLS no. 103B, p. 351

Is any of you so eager for knowledge and the beneficent powers it confers as to be ready to leave your world and come into ours? Then let him come; but he must not think to return until the seal of the mysteries has locked his lips even against the chances of his own weakness or indiscretion. Let him come by all means, as the pupil to the master, and without conditions; or let him wait, as so many others have, and be satisfied with such crumbs of knowledge as may fall in his way.

To: APS   **From:** KH   **Date:** October 19, 1880   MLS no. 2, p. 8

So, my good brother, be not surprised, and blame us not as readily as you have already done, at any development of our policy towards the aspirants past, present or future. Only those who can look ahead at the far remote consequences of things are in a position to judge as to the expediency of our own actions, or those we permit in others. What may seem present bad faith may in the end prove the truest, most benevolent loyalty. Let time show who was right and who faithless.

To: APS   **From:** KH   **Date:** ca. October 1882   MLS no. 92, p. 299

P. Sreenivasrow is in great mental distress once more because of my long silence, not having a clear intuition developed (as how should he after the life he has led?). He fears he is abandoned, whereas he has not been lost sight of for one moment. From day to day he is making his own record at the "Ashrum," from night to night receiving instructions fitted to his spiritual capabilities.

To: HSO   **From:** KH   **Date:** ca. August 1888   1 LMW no. 19, p. 51

To yourself personally, child, struggling thro' darkness to the Light, I would say, that the Path is *never* closed; but in proportion to one's previous errors so is it harder to find and to tread. In the eyes of the "Master" no one is ever "utterly condemned." As the lost jewel may be recovered from the very depths of the tank's mud, so can the most abandoned snatch himself from the mire of sin, if only the precious Gem of Gems, the sparkling germ of the Atma, is developed. Each of us must do *that* for himself, each *can* if he but will and persevere.

To: FA   **From:** KH   **Date:** ca. Fall 1884   1 LMW no. 20, p. 56

My dear sir, we neither want men to rush on blind-fold, nor are we prepared to abandon tried friends—*who rather pass for fools* than reveal what they may have learnt under a solemn pledge of never revealing it unless permitted—even for the chance of getting men of the very *highest* class—nor are we especially anxious to have anyone work for us except with entire spontaneity. We want true and unselfish hearts; fearless and confiding souls, and are quite willing to leave the men of the "higher class" and far higher intellects to grope their own way to the light.

To: AOH   **From:** KH   **Date:** ca. December 1880   MLS no. 11, p. 34

In point of fact, there is nowhere in physical nature a mountain abyss so hopelessly impassable and obstructive to the traveler as that spiritual one, which keeps them back from me.

To: APS and AOH   **From:** KH via M   **Date:** ca. October 1881   MLS no. 29, p. 87

To sum up: the misuse of knowledge by the pupil always reacts upon the initiator; nor do I believe you know yet, that in sharing his secrets with another the Adept, by an immutable Law, is delaying his own progress to the Eternal Rest. Perhaps, what I now tell you may help you to a truer conception of things, and to appreciate our mutual position the better. Loitering on the way does not conduce to a speedy arrival at the journey's end. And, it must strike you as a truism that a *Price* must be paid for every thing and every truth by *somebody*, and in this case—WE pay it.

To: APS   **From:** KH   **Date:** August 5, 1881   MLS no. 20, p. 74

They [C. C. Massey, H. Hood, S. Moses] were all tried and tested in various ways, and not one of them came up [to] the desired mark. M. gave a special attention to "C.C.M." for reasons I will now explain, and, with results as at present known to you. You may say that such a secret way of testing people is *dishonest*; that we ought to have warned him, etc. Well, all I can say is, that it may be so from your European standpoint, but that, being Asiatics, we cannot depart from our rules. A man's character, his true inner nature can never be thoroughly drawn out if he believes himself watched, or strives for an object.

To: APS   **From:** KH   **Date:** ca. October 1882   MLS no. 92, p. 298

You know our motto, and that its practical application has erased the word "impossible" from the occultist's vocabulary. If he wearies not of trying, he may discover that most noble of all facts, his true SELF. But he will have to penetrate many strata before he comes to It. And to begin with let him rid himself of the *maya* that any man living can set up "claims" upon Adepts. He may create irresistible attractions and compel their attention, but they will be spiritual, not mental or intellectual . . . Once separated from the common influences of society, nothing draws us to any outsider save his evolving spirituality.

To: APS   **From:** KH   **Date:** July 1883   MLS no. 111, p. 374

My good friend—it is very easy for us to give phenomenal proofs when we have necessary conditions. For instance—Olcott's magnetism after six years of purification is intensely sympathetic with ours—physically and morally is constantly becoming more and more so. Damodar and Bhavani Rao being congenitally sympathetic their auras help—instead of repelling and impeding phenomenal experiments. After a time you may become so—it depends on yourself. To force phenomena in the presence of difficulties magnetic and other is forbidden, as strictly as for a bank cashier to disburse money which is only entrusted to him.

To: APS   **From:** KH   **Date:** March 11, 1882   MLS no. 50, p. 143

Though you may have read in the modern works on mes-
merism how that which we call "Will-Essence"—and you
"fluid"—is transmitted from the operator to his objective
point, you perhaps scarcely realize how everyone is practically, albeit unconsciously, demonstrating this law every
day and every moment. Nor, can you quite realize how
the training for adeptship increases both one's capacity
to emit and to feel this form of force. I assure you that I,
though but a humble chela as yet, felt your good wishes
flowing to me as the convalescent in the cold mountains
feels from the gentle breeze that blows upon him from the
plains below.

To: APS   **From:** DK   **Date:** ca. January 1882   MLS no. 37, p. 106

Him [HSO] we can trust under all circumstances, and his
faithful service is pledged to us come well, come ill. My
dear Brother, my voice is the echo of impartial justice.
Where can we find an equal devotion? He is one who
never questions, but obeys; who may make innumerable mistakes out of excessive zeal but never is unwilling
to repair his fault even at the cost of the greatest self-
humiliation; who esteems the sacrifice of comfort and
even life something to be cheerfully risked whenever
necessary; who will eat any food, or even go without;
sleep on any bed, work in any place, fraternise with any
outcast, endure any privation for the cause.

To: APS   **From:** KH   **Date:** November 3, 1880   MLS no. 5, p. 17

By placing so constantly her personality over above her inner and better Self—tho' she knows it not—she [LCH] has done all she could for the last week to sever herself from us for ever. Yet so pure and genuine she is that I am ready to leave a chink in the door she slams unconsciously to herself into her own face, and await for the entire awakening of the honest nature whenever that time comes. She is without artifice or malice, entirely truthful and sincere, yet at times quite false to herself. As she says, her ways are not *our* ways, nor can she comprehend them. Her personality coming in so strong in her ideas of the fitness of things, she cannot certainly understand our acts on our plane of life.

To: FA   **From:** KH   **Date:** ca. Fall 1884   1 LMW no. 20, p. 53

You offer your services; well. You are willing to devote time, incur expense, run risks for OUR cause. Well, it is the cause of humanity, of true religion, of education, of enlightenment and spiritual elevation, of course. It needs missionaries, devotees, agents, even martyrs perhaps. But it cannot demand of *any* man to make himself either. If he so chooses—well; well for the world and for himself. For, to work for mankind is grand, its recompense stretches beyond this brief dream of life into other births. So now, you my chela, choose and grasp your own destiny. You wish to heal the sick—do so; but remember your success will be measured by *your faith*—in yourself, more than in us. Lose it for a second, and failure will follow.

To: S. Ramaswamier   **From:** M   **Date:** ca. October 1882   2 LMW no. 51, p. 97

Relationships Between Adepts and Chelas   77

We—the criticized and misunderstood Brothers—we seek to bring men to sacrifice their personality—a passing flash—for the welfare of the whole humanity, hence for their own *immortal* Egos, a part of the latter, as humanity is a fraction of the integral whole, that it will one day become . . . we—leave it to our menials—the *dugpas* [sorcerers] at our service, by giving them *carte blanche* for the time being, and with the sole object of drawing out the whole *inner* nature of the chela, most of the nooks and corners of which would remain dark and concealed for ever, were not an opportunity afforded to test each of these corners in turn. Whether the chela wins or loses the prize—depends solely on himself.

To: AOH   **From:** KH   **Date:** ca. August 1882   MLS no. 74, p. 222

I cannot control a feeling of repugnance to going into particulars about this, that, and the other [occult] phenomenon that may have occurred. They are the playthings of the tyro and if we sometimes have gratified the craving for them . . . we do not feel called upon to be continually explaining away deceptive appearances, due to mixed carelessness and credulity, or blind skepticism, as the case may be. For the present we offer our knowledge—some portions of it at least—to be either accepted or rejected on its own merits independently—entirely so—from the source from which it emanates. In return, we ask neither allegiance, loyalty, nor even simple courtesy—nay, we [would] rather have nothing of the sort offered since we would have to decline the kind offer.

To: APS   **From:** KH   **Date:** ca. January 1883   MLS no. 103B, p. 352

It is, as though a child should ask me to teach him the highest problems of Euclid before he had even begun studying the elementary rules of arithmetic. Only the progress one makes in the study of Arcane knowledge from its rudimental elements, brings him gradually to understand our meaning. Only thus, and not otherwise, does it, strengthening and refining those mysterious links of sympathy between intelligent men—the temporarily isolated fragments of the universal Soul and the cosmic Soul itself—bring them into full rapport. Once this established, then only will these awakened sympathies serve, indeed, to connect MAN with . . . that energetic chain which binds together the material and Immaterial Kosmos, Past, Present, and Future, and quicken his perceptions so as to clearly grasp, not merely all things of matter, but of Spirit also.

To: APS   **From:** KH   **Date:** February 20, 1881   MLS no. 15, p. 46

Alone the adepts, i.e., the embodied spirits—are forbidden by our wise and intransgressible laws to completely subject to themselves another and a weaker will—that of free born man. The latter mode of proceeding is the favourite one resorted to by the "Brothers of the Shadow," the Sorcerers.

To: APS   **From:** KH   **Date:** July 5, 1881   MLS no. 18, p. 59

Nature has linked all parts of her Empire together by subtle threads of magnetic sympathy, and there is a mutual correlation even between a star and a man; thought runs swifter than the electric fluid, and your thought *will find me* if projected by a pure impulse, as mine will find, has found, and often impressed your mind. We may move in cycles of activity divided—not entirely separated from each other. Like the light in the sombre valley seen by the mountaineer from his peaks, every bright thought in your mind, my Brother, will sparkle and attract the attention of your distant friend and correspondent. If thus we discover our natural Allies in the *Shadow*-world—your world and ours outside the precincts—and it is our law to approach every such an one if even there be but the feeblest glimmer of the true "Tathagata" light within him—then how far easier for you to attract us.

To: APS   **From:** KH   **Date:** ca. February 1882   MLS no. 47, p. 132

Meanwhile—remember: it is because we are playing a risky game and the stakes are human souls that I ask you to possess yours in patience. Bearing in mind that I have to look after your "Soul" and mine too, I propose to do so at whatever cost, even at the risk of being misunderstood by you.

To: APS   **From:** KH   **Date:** July 5, 1881   MLS no. 15, p. 58

When you are older in your chela life you will not be surprised if no notice is taken of your wishes, and even birthdays and other feasts and fasts. For you will have then learned to put a proper value on the carcass-sheath of the Self and all its relations. To the profane a birthday is but a twelve-month stride towards the grave. When each new year marks for you a step of evolution, all will be ready with their congratulations; there will be something real to felicitate you upon. But, so far, you are not even one year old—and you would be treated as an adult! Try to learn to stand firm on your legs, child, before you venture walking. It is because you are so young and ignorant in the ways of occult life that you are so easily forgiven. But you have to attend ours ways and put L.C.H. and her caprices and whims far in the background before the expiration of the first year of your life as a chela if you would see the dawn of the second year.

To: LCH   **From:** KH   **Date:** August 22, 1884   1 LMW no. 30 p. 72

I deeply regret it, but have no right to bind myself so securely to any person or persons by ties of personal sympathy and esteem that my movements shall be crippled, and I unable to lead the rest to something grander and nobler than their present faith. Therefore, I choose to leave him in his present errors.

To: APS   **From:** KH   **Date:** January 6, 1883   MLS no. 101, p. 342

Now, if we allow of different aspects or portions of the Whole Truth being visible to different agencies or intelligences, each under various conditions, as for example various portions of the one landscape develop themselves to various persons, at various distances and from various standpoints—if we admit the fact of various or different agencies (individual Brothers for instance) endeavouring to develop the *Egos* of different individuals, without subjecting entirely their wills to their own (as it is forbidden) but by availing themselves of their physical, moral, and intellectual idiosyncracies; if we add to this the countless kosmical influences which distort and deflect all efforts to achieve definite purposes: if we remember, moreover, the direct hostility of the Brethren of the Shadow always on the watch to perplex and haze the neophyte's brain, I think we shall have no difficulty in understanding how even a definite spiritual advance may to a certain extent lead different individuals to apparently different conclusions and theories.

To: APS　　**From:** KH　　**Date:** July 5, 1881　　MLS no. 18, p. 67

I will not tell you to give up this or that, for unless you exhibit *beyond any doubt* the presence in you of the necessary *germs* [for chelaship] it would be as useless as it would be cruel. But I say—TRY. Do not despair.

To: APS　　**From:** KH　　**Date:** December 1, 1880　　MLS no. 10, p. 27

It is a familiar saying that a well matched couple "grow together," so as to come to a close resemblance in features as well as in mind. But do you know that between adept and chela—master and pupil—there gradually forms a closer tie; for the psychic interchange is regulated scientifically, whereas between husband and wife unaided nature is left to herself. As the water in a full tank runs into an empty one which it is connected with; and as the common level will be sooner or later reached according to the capacity of the feedpipe, so does the knowledge of the adept flow to the chela; and the chela attains the adept level according to his receptive capacities. At the same time the chela being an individual, a separate evolution, unconsciously imparts to the master the quality of his accumulated mentality. The master absorbs *his* knowledge; and if it is a question of language he does not know, the master will get the chela's linguistic accumulations just as they are—idioms and all—unless he takes the trouble to sift and remodel the phrases when using.

To: AOH   **From:** KH   **Date:** ca. 1882   1 LMW no. 43, p. 93

Try. Seek and ye will find. Ask and it will be given ye. Use your will power and may the benediction of Truth and the Divine Presence of Him the Inscrutable be upon thee and help thee to open thy intuition.

To: HSO   **From:** SB   **Date:** ca. June 1875   2 LMW no. 10, p. 29

And though we neither push nor draw into the mysterious domain of occult nature those who are unwilling; never shrink from expressing our opinions freely and fearlessly, yet we are ever as ready to assist those who come to us; even to—*agnostics* who assume the negative position of *"knowing nothing but phenomena and refuse to believe in anything else."* It is true that the married man cannot be an adept, yet without striving to become "a Raja Yogi" he can acquire certain powers and do as much good to mankind and often more, by remaining within the precincts of this world of his. Therefore, shall we not ask you to precipitately change fixed habits of life, before the full conviction of its necessity and advantage has possessed you. You are a man to be left to lead himself and may be so left with safety. Your resolution is taken to deserve much: time will effect the rest. There are more ways than one for acquiring occult knowledge. "Many are the grains of incense destined for one and the same altar: one falls sooner into the fire, the other later—the difference of time is nothing," remarked a great man when he was refused admission and supreme initiation into the mysteries.

To: APS   From: KH   Date: November 3, 1880   MLS no. 5, p. 19

As Subba Row has explained to you, the aim of the philanthropist should be the spiritual enlightenment of his fellow-men, and whoever works unselfishly to that goal necessarily puts himself in magnetic communication with our chelas and *ourselves*.

To: Ootamram   From: KH   Date: March 1884   1 LMW no. 44, p. 100
Trivedi

Why is it that doubts and foul suspicions seem to beset every aspirant for chelaship? My friend, in the Masonic Lodges of old times the neophyte was subjected to a series of frightful tests of his constancy, courage and presence of mind. By psychological impressions supplemented by machinery and chemicals, he was made to believe himself falling down precipices, crushed by rocks, walking spider-web bridges in mid-air, passing through fire, drowned in water and attacked by wild beasts. This was a reminiscence of and a programme borrowed from the Egyptian Mysteries. The West having lost the secrets of the East, had, as I say, to resort to artifice. But in these days the vulgarization of science has rendered such trifling tests obsolete. The aspirant is now assailed entirely on the psychological side of his nature. His course of testing—in Europe and India—is that of Raj-yog and its result is—as frequently explained—to develop every germ good and bad in him in his temperament. The rule is inflexible, and not one escapes whether he but writes to us a letter, or in the privacy of his own heart's thought formulates a strong desire for occult communication and knowledge. As the shower cannot fructify the rock, so the occult teaching has no effect upon the unreceptive mind; and as the water develops the heat of caustic lime so does the teaching bring into fierce action every unsuspected potentiality latent in him.

To: APS   **From:** KH   **Date:** ca. Spring 1885   MLS no. 136, p. 451

I am also of opinion that few candidates imagine the degree of inconvenience—nay suffering and harm to himself—the said initiator [Adept] submits to for the sake of his pupil. The peculiar physical, moral, and intellectual conditions of neophytes and Adepts alike vary much, as anyone will easily understand; thus, in each case, the instructor has to adapt his conditions to those of the pupil, and the strain is terrible, for to achieve success we have to bring ourselves into a *full* rapport with the subject under training. And as the greater the powers of the Adept the less he is in sympathy with the natures of the profane who often come to him saturated with the emanations of the outside world, those animal emanations of the selfish, brutal, crowd that we so dread—the longer he was separated from that world and the purer he has himself become, the more difficult the self-imposed task. Then—knowledge can only be communicated gradually; and some of the highest secrets—if actually formulated even in your well prepared ear—might sound to you as insane gibberish, notwithstanding all the sincerity of your present assurance that "absolute trust defies misunderstanding." This is the real cause of our reticence. This is why people so often complain with a plausible show of reason that no new knowledge is communicated to them, though they have toiled for it for two, three or more years. Let those who really desire to learn *abandon all* and come to us, instead of asking or expecting us to go to them.

To: APS   **From:** KH   **Date:** August 5, 1881   MLS no. 20, p. 73

Your strivings, perplexities and forebodings are equally noticed, good and faithful friend. In the imperishable RECORD of the Masters *you have written them all.* There are registered your every deed and thought; for, though not a chela, as you say to my Brother Morya, nor even a "protégé"—as you understand the term—still, you have stepped within the circle of our work, you have crossed the mystic line which separates your world from ours, and now whether you persevere or not; whether we become later on, in your sight, still more living *real* entities or vanish out of your mind like so many dream fictions— perchance an ugly night-mare—you are virtually OURS. Your hidden *Self* has mirrored itself in *our* Akasa; your nature is—yours, your essence is—ours. The flame is distinct from the log of wood which serves it temporarily as fuel; at the end of your apparitional birth—and whether we two meet face to face in our grosser *rupas*—you cannot avoid meeting us in *Real Existence.* Yea, verily good friend your *Karma* is ours, for you imprinted it daily and hourly upon the pages of that book where the minutest particulars of the individuals stepping inside our circle— are preserved; and that your *Karma* is your *only* personality to be when you step beyond. In thought and deed, by day, in soul-struggles by nights, you have been writing the story of your desires and your spiritual development. This, every one does who approaches us with any earnestness of desire to become our co-worker; he himself "precipitates" the written entries by the identical process used by us when we write inside your closed letters and uncut pages of books and pamphlets in transit.

To: APS   **From:** KH   **Date:** ca. February 1882   MLS no. 47, p. 131

Further Resources

For those who are serious in pursuing advancement on the higher spiritual path, up to and including chelaship of an Adept, there are other useful and publicly accessible, or nonproprietary, works on this subject besides *The Mahatma Letters to A. P. Sinnett* and *Letters from the Masters of the Wisdom,* in which most excerpts in this book can be found. Because many of these works appear in various editions and in numerous printings, what is given here are simply the title and author. It is left to the wayfarer to identify the particular publisher, edition, and printing of those books he or she may wish to acquire.

Foremost is *Light on the Path* by Mabel Collins. Another book by Mabel Collins, viewed by some as a companion book to *Light on the Path,* is *When the Sun Moves Northward.*

Two small works by H. P. Blavatsky are most useful as guidebooks: *The Voice of the Silence* and *Practical Occultism.* See also two articles published by her in early numbers of *The Theosophist* and reprinted in *H. P. Blavatsky Collected Writings*: "Chelas and Lay Chelas" (vol. 4, 1888, p. 606) and "Chelas" (vol. 6, 1883–1885, p. 285).

Another informative guide for chelaship appears as chapter 10, "The Occult Hierarchy," in *Man: Fragments of Forgotten History,* written by two chelas of Koot Hoomi—Laura Holloway and Mohini Chatterjee.

Finally, serious seekers should consult the five "E. S. [Esoteric Section] Instructions" promulgated by H. P. B. that appear in vol. 12, 1889–1890, of *H. P. Blavatsky Collected Writings* (pp. 515–713) and H. P. B.'s *The Secret Doctrine Dialogues*, published in 2014 by The Theosophy Company.

Mention should also be made of two other works that, though not endorsed by everyone, contain some useful information and guidance: *At the Feet of the Master* by J. Krishnamurti and *The Masters and the Path* by C. W. Leadbeater.

W. W. Q.

About the Author

William Wilson Quinn has been a serious student of the *philosophia perennis* since 1968, and is a practitioner of those of its principles that guide one's life toward greater spiritual awareness and truth. He is an alumnus of the University of Chicago, where he earned the M.A. from the Divinity School, and the Ph.D. from the Division of Humanities. He also earned a J.D. degree, and practiced law for several decades. He is the author of three books and over 50 articles published in various national and international journals.

www.ingramcontent.com/pod-product-compliance
Lightning Source LLC
Chambersburg PA
CBHW022011080426

42733CB00007B/568